The
Fortunate
Child

Maxine Sue Feller

L.A. Times recommended *"Don't Call Me Mama"*
and this book is the *sequel*

508 West 26th Street KEARNEY, NE 68848
402-819-3224
info@medialiteraryexcellence.com

CONTENTS

ACKNOWLEDGMENTS

After an accident, in 2018 it was suggested I write a book about my life to enable me to review it… perhaps understand myself better. "DON'T CALL ME MAMA "was published in Spring of 2021, and the Los Angeles Times reviewed it and said it was a "good summer read".

Recently, I was sad to read the suicide rate of teens and young adults has risen significantly. Friends suggested that I write a sequel of the story to inspire those who might be thinking it would be better not to continue to live on with the struggle to realize one must overcome difficulties to become a strong adult…Living requires effort. A diamond becomes one because the pressures put upon the rock turns it into a diamond.

Thank you to all the negative and positive people in my life who contributed to my journey to survive. A special thanks to Robbin and Shaiya Schenker whose love and creativity crafted the cover.

CHAPTER 1

After I read, "The milestones in the life of a person are birth, school, graduation, work, marriage, divorce, death, or retirement," in the epilogue of Joseph Campbell's book, "The Hero With A Thousand Faces," I was very surprised.

Until that moment I'd thought that the milestones of my life were incidents that caused the more dramatic changes.

The earliest memory I recall began on a June morning in 1936 when I was awakened by Mama's voice, screaming up the staircase to the second-floor bedroom, "Wake up, Max! My brother is here waiting to take you along with him."

I really liked being with my nine-year old Uncle Larry. It meant having fun. Quickly, I jumped out of bed, washed and pulled on my over-sized sun suit. Then, holding onto the wooden banister, I hurried downstairs and ran through the living room to the kitchen.

Mama handed me a slice of bread and butter, and Uncle Larry hoisted me, his three-year old niece onto his shoulders. Mama opened the door for us. I waived to my "sissy cousin" Melvin who was eating breakfast at the kitchen table with his mother.

Larry always took me, and not him. Larry loves me I thought as we hurried to the street corner where the neighborhood boys were waiting for us. I clung to his neck.

"Here comes Larry," one of them, the tall brown-shirted Otto said, and passed the brown bag of candy that he always brought with him to Larry.

"What are we doing for fun today?" Larry asked.

Otto was wearing his usual brown shirt, and stroked his yellow hair. He rubbed his chin and said, "We're going to throw snowballs."

I was very surprised to hear him say that. It was a sunny day in June, and there was no snow on the ground.

"Dum ta dum" the boys chanted as they galloped after him on their imaginary horses. Then, Otto stopped in front of a big wooden house. Hydrangea bushes were growing on the lawn next to the house. They covered the bushes with their large white flowers. I was amazed. They really did look like snowballs.

Larry put me down on the lawn. Otto tore off one of the blossoms and said, "Add pebbles to these 'snowballs,' and we'll throw them at the people who pass by."

I pulled off a flower too, but I didn't add the pebbles to it. We hurled them at two teenaged girls who were walking by.

"Ouch!" they cried and ran away. Then the boys all laughed at the girls.

Next, I saw a lady holding her child by the hand coming toward us. I didn't think that the boys would throw anything at her, but I was wrong. They pelted her with "snowballs".

The brave woman raised her arm and pointed to Otto who was the oldest in the group. She shouted, "You Nazis are a bad influence on these children!"

Otto pulled off another snowball and was lacing it with pebbles to throw at her. Suddenly, the front door opened and a burly man dressed in an undershirt and pants came outside. Otto screamed, "Yipes!" He dropped his snowball and ran. All the boys ran after him, and I did too.

The owner of the house bounded down his front steps and chased after us. The man caught me by my sun suit's straps, and spun me around. I saw him raise his hairy arm to hit me, and scrunched my eyes shut in anticipation of what was to come.

When no blow landed on me, I peeked and saw he had lowered his arm. He shook his head and said, "I no hit babies" and walked back into his house.

Feeling insulted at being called a baby I stamped my foot on the sidewalk and shouted, "I'm no baby! I know where I live" and then I walked home.

***

I waited in the house a long time for Larry to return. I wanted him to read to me in the front room. I was passing the time looking at the pictures in the Grimm's "Fairy Tales" book. Larry had read these stories to me many times. I knew them by heart, but I enjoyed sitting close beside him.

Larry arrived and asked, "Are you okay, Max?" Seated on the couch I nodded my head.

He said, "We were worried about leaving you. Come outside and show the boys that you're all right."

As we walked from the living room through the kitchen to the back porch I realized no one had stayed to see what happened to me. When Larry pushed open the door screen we stood in the doorway. and I looked down at the upturned faces.

"Max, what happened?" they asked.

Well, I wasn't going to tell them the man said I'm a baby, and then let go of me. They might call me baby too… I quickly made up a story. "The man caught me. I raised my fists and shouted, "You let me go, or I'll hit you!" And the man let me go."

On hearing my heroic tale the boys murmured in wonder. However, Otto shouted, "Nah! He let her go 'cause she's a girl."

I thought to be called a girl was worse than being called a baby. "I'm no girl!"

Some of the boys snickered. Otto jeered. "Go ask your Mama if you don't believe me," he said, and then they all laughed.

Upset, I opened the screen door and ran inside to search for my mother. I found her on her knees scrubbing the bathroom floor tiles with some nasty smelling stuff.

"Am I a girl?"

Surprised by my question she stopped what she was doing, and sat looking up at me. "Of course you're a girl, Maxine."

I stamped my foot, "No! I'm not a girl. Uncle Larry takes me to be with the boys."

"Larry takes care of you while I do the housework, Maxine. Tonight, when I bathe you and Melvin, I'll show you why you're not a boy."

***

That evening Mama placed me in the tub first, and then dangled Melvin's body in front of my face. I saw he had something between his legs that I didn't have. *Hmm. I don't have that thing between my legs. Is that what makes him a boy? If it comes off, can I put it on me?*

When Mama left us to get a bath towel. I grabbed his boy thing and tried to yank it loose.

"Ow-w!" he wailed.

It didn't come off. So, I had to agree that I must be a girl. Hmm. *Tomorrow, I'll stay in the house and see what girls do for fun.*

CHAPTER 2

In the morning, I washed, and dressed. From downstairs I overheard Mama, Aunt Jean, and Grandma talking in the kitchen. When I entered the room Mama giggled and pointed at me. "Max thought she was a boy!" Then the women all laughed.

Mama had squealed on me! Furious, I saw red and charged at her. I hit and kicked her with all my might. Everyone stopped laughing. Mama grabbed my arm and held it behind my back then she forced me to walk back upstairs.

After that she unlocked the dreaded hall closet… Grandma had told me a monster lived inside it. She pushed me into it, and locked the door. "You'll stay in there until your father comes home."

I was scared the monster was going to hurt me. It was very dark in there. Terrified, I banged on the door. "Let me out!" In the blackness I felt something touch my head. *The closet monster wants to eat me!* I fought it back until it no longer dared to touch me. Exhausted, hungry, and thirsty I pounded on the door. "Let me out."

No one came to open the door. I had to pee and wailed, "It's no fun to be a girl." Then, I fell asleep.

***

Daddy came home and the closet was unlocked. Their angry voices awakened me. I rubbed my eyes and saw there was no monster lying on the floor beside me. Strewn about me were shredded shirts and dresses. *Grandma hadn't told me the truth.*

Mama was shouting, "See what a monster your daughter is. You must punish her!"

My six-foot, two-inch Daddy plucked me from the closet. I was frightened as he carried me into the bedroom and closed the door. Then he put me down and unfastened his leather belt. *He's going to whip me with it I thought.* I whimpered, "Daddy, I want to be just like you."

He folded his belt in half, and knelt beside me and whispered, "When I snap my belt, you cry out like I'm hurting you."

I didn't understand what he'd told me to do. Daddy made a snapping noise with the belt. "Cry out," he encouraged me, and he snapped his belt again.

"Ouch! Wha-a!" I screamed, making believe Daddy was hurting me.

On the other side of the door, I heard Mama laughing. She said, "That's it! Hit her some more."

I was very sad she was happy to think Daddy was hurting me. He snapped the belt several times. I shed real tears on hearing Mama's laughter. *Mama is not my friend.* I was glad we were fooling her. I decided Daddy was my friend, and hugged his legs. I didn't speak to Mama for a long time.

CHAPTER 3

It was decided Melvin and I should no longer be bathed together. Mama washed him first. Then, she lowered me into his dirty bath water and soaped up a wash- cloth to clean me. I did not like that.

***

Several nights later in the dirty tub I asked, "Mama, why don't you paint your finger nails?"

She chuckled. "Who have you seen that wears nail polish?"

"The blonde lady Daddy takes me to see when we go out on Sunday."

Mama stopped washing me, and screamed, "Ma!"

I heard my Grandma huffing and puffing as she pulled her overweight body up the steps. She entered the bathroom and panted, "What's wrong?"

Mama shouted, "Maxine, tell her what you just told me!"

I didn't think I'd said anything to get her upset, but I was hesitant to repeat it. Then Mama shook me. "Tell her", she said again and slapped me across the face.

Weeping, I repeated what I'd said, and they left me sitting alone in the bathroom.

***

Uncle Larry came upstairs to dry me off, and put me to bed. As he tucked me in, I asked, "What's wrong?"

He said, "You did a bad thing."

"What did I do?"

"You're a snitch. You squealed on your father. Nothing will ever be the same in this house again."

"Do you still love me?" He didn't answer me. Frightened and crying, I pulled the blanket over my three-year-old head, and soon fell asleep.

Later that night I was awakened by something that had been dropped on the foot of my bed. Rubbing the sleep from my eyes I sat up and saw it was a suitcase. Mama was screaming at my Daddy, "You get out of this house!"

He took his clothes from the dresser and dropped them into the open case. He didn't say a word. He closed the lid and locked it. Then, he carried it out of the room. But Daddy gave me no signal to come along with him as he usually did when Mama yelled at him.

I jumped out of bed and ran to the open window and shouted, "Daddy!" I thought he'd forgotten me. I was hoping he'd come back to get me. But, he got into his car parked in front of the house, and drove away. He didn't even wave "goodbye "to me.

I was unhappy to be left with my angry Mama. She snarled, "See! He doesn't love you any more either. You be good, or I'll throw you out too!"

Where would I go? Daddy could go to my other Grandma's house, but where would I go if Mama threw me out?" I pulled the blanket over my head and fell asleep whimpering softly.

CHAPTER 4

I awoke the next morning and went downstairs. Blocking the kitchen door was Grandma. She placed a finger at the side of her nose and said, "Little pitchers have big ears." I understood her to mean I was a snitch, and was no longer welcome in her kitchen.

Sadly, I shuffled to the living room and sat on the floor. I looked at the pictures in the books. After I finished, I looked out the front window at the people passing by. *Where are they going?* I wondered, and I wished that I could go there too.

***

Some days I would sit on the concrete stoop steps in front of our house and look at my picture books, or play games with my stuffed animals. Often, a very long black car would park at the curb and stay for a long time. I saw that a man and a woman sat in the rear of the car smiling as they watched me at play.

***

I was sitting on the stone stairs sobbing one day, when the car came again. This time the man was alone. He saw that I was crying, and got out of his car. He walked up to me. He was wearing a white suit and a straw hat. He asked me, "Why are you crying?"

I didn't tell him that Mama had just shouted at me, "You're just like your father. One day, I'll throw you out, too!" Instead, I told him that I wanted an ice cream cone.

"Come and walk to the corner store with me, and I'll buy one for you." I took his hand and went with him. He asked me what flavor I wanted.

"Chocolate, please."

He bought a cone for me, and I licked it. He asked, "Are you happy now?"

I sighed deeply and lied, "Yes… thank you."

The man walked me back to my house and knocked on the door. Grandma opened the door, and he went inside to speak with her and Mama. I sat enjoying the cool ice cream. It did make me feel better.

When he came out he pat me on the head, said "Goodbye and good luck" and then he got into the backseat of his car, and it drove away.

***

The following day, workmen arrived to install a wire fence around the front of our house. I watched them at work with great interest while I sat inside at the window. It was much later that I learned "the kind man" was a wealthy, childless man who had offered to adopt me.

Mama had refused him. Fearing that man might try to steal me Grandma decided to have a fence installed to prevent me from being taken by him.

CHAPTER 5

Uncle Larry came to me one day and said, "Otto says you can join the gang if you'll do what he asks you to do."

My cousin Melvin had been going out with Larry to meet with the boys and play. I was glad for a chance to be with the boys again. It was just no fun to sit around the house alone day after day.

Although I was allowed to go into the basement where Grandma lived with her two sons, because I helped lift the one pound, and later five-pound weights onto the bar of my Uncle Al who was practicing to pose for a weight lifting photo magazine

We walked up the street to the boys on the corner. Otto grinned, "Max, boys are better than girls. Boys are strong. Do you think that you're strong?" I nodded my head, and heard some of the boys snickering.

"Do you want to be in my gang?"

I nodded again, and he chuckled. "Well, if you can punch one of my boys and make him bleed, then you can join the gang. Okay?" I nodded again.

Otto ordered the boys to line up so I could pick out one to punch. Slowly, I walked along in front of the line of boys. They were taller than me. It would be foolish of me to pick a tall boy to punch.

I stopped in front of my cousin, Melvin. He was only a little bigger than me. He and his Mom and Dad lived in the rear bedroom on the same floor with my Mom and me. I recalled overhearing Aunt Jean complain Melvin had a weak nose. So, I clenched my fist and punched him on the nose as hard as any four-year-old could. who had been lifting one-and-five-pound weights.

To my delight, and the surprise of the group, blood spurted out of his nose. Melvin ran home crying, "Mama."

Otto scowled. "A girl can't be in my gang." he said, and walked away. It was then that I understood he'd meant to have me be "the fun of the day."

The boys were not laughing. "She did it fair and square," one of them said. They talked it over for a few minutes and decided that I should be allowed to join. Then they all patted me on the back, and welcomed me as a new member to the group.

However, as Larry walked me home, I wondered if I wanted to be friends with boys who had wanted to laugh at me. *Hmm.*

***

We entered the house and I overheard Aunt Jean shouting at my mother, "Maxine is a hooligan. Look what she did to my son."

Larry whispered in my ear, "Melvin's a snitch. He can't be in our gang anymore."

***

Not long after this incident, Larry took me to the big yellow brick house where Otto lived. We entered through the driveway-side door and walked into a wood-paneled room. There was a photograph of a man with a small moustache, and a red flag with a white circle in the middle, and a black spider sitting on it that hung on a long wall.

Otto stood next to a desk piled high with printed papers. His gang of boys surrounded him. He called each boy by name, and gave him a stack of papers to hand out on various street corners. I wondered what task Otto had in mind for me to do.

After the boys were gone, Otto unbuckled his pants and pulled down his under-clothes below his knees. He took hold of his boy thing and said, "If you want to be in my gang, Max come here and open your mouth."

To be in his gang I have to do what Otto says, but he wants to pee in my mouth. Yuck! I decided to run out the door and back to my house.

I didn't tell anyone about what had happened. However, when Larry came home the next day with a black eye, I thought it was my fault that he got hit.

I was unaware the pamphlets handed out were anti-semitic Nazi propaganda suggesting Jews be punished. Larry never told Grandma why he was being hit after school. Often, he would sit in the cold winter air wearing only his shirt and shivering with the cold.

CHAPTER 6

At dinner, I overheard Mama say to Grandma she was "divorcing her husband." I didn't know what that meant.

After dinner, I asked Larry, "What's a divorce?"

He explained to me my father wasn't going to sleep in this house anymore. "Your mother will have to go out and find herself a job."

I was disappointed my Daddy hadn't taken me with him when he left. I thought he went to live with my other Grandma. Then, I remembered that I'd snitched on him. *Oh, he didn't take me because he's mad at me. The divorce is my fault.* I was glad Larry still loved me, and he could explain to me what was happening around here.

***

Mama opened a letter that had come to the house. She read it to Grandma, "The divorce decree is final." Then, I saw her tear the letter into little pieces.

Grandma said, "Maxine, go outside and play." I dawdled and overheard her say to Mama, "It's easy for a man to re-marry. He has no baggage left with him. It won't be as easy for you. Larry is six years older than Maxine. It will be better for you to say that she is my child."

That night while Mama was bathing me she said, "Maxine, don't call me Mama anymore."

I thought, *Mama must be mad at me. It's my fault Daddy doesn't sleep here anymore. I'm a squealer. Now, she doesn't want to be my mother.* I was brokenhearted.

As she dried me she said, "From now on call me "Yetta." I want you to call Grandma your "Mama." Don't ask me any questions, or tell anyone about what I'm telling you now. Just do as I say, and never tell any neighbors what goes on in our house."

Later, in my bed, I kept thinking, *Mama doesn't want me anymore. I'm a bad girl, and* I cried myself to sleep.

CHAPTER 7

One day a package arrived at the house. I was very excited, and curious.

"Mama who is it for?"

Grandma said, "When Yetta comes home she'll open it up and tell us." As she was preparing the evening meal my mother came home from work. Grandma said, "A package came to the house. Who sent it?"

My mother opened the package. Inside, I saw a coloring book, a letter, and a box of crayons. "It's a gift for Maxine from her father."

On hearing this, I clapped my hands and danced around the room. *Daddy had stopped being mad at me.*

My mother read the letter in the box. She had a funny smile on her face while she said. "Maxine, you don't want to stay with your father over the Christmas holidays", and shook her head "No" while she was asking me.

Jewish people didn't celebrate Christmas. Grandma lit candles each Friday night before sundown, and covered her head and said a prayer. Although I'd been born into a Jewish household, they didn't seriously practice their religion, or attend a synagogue; except for three high holy days. They didn't practice Jewish traditions, but they spoke Yiddish.

"Oh goodie!" I said.

The smile left my mother's face, and she glared at me. *I was sorry about the divorce, and that she had to go to work. I wished many times I'd never asked her why she didn't paint her nails.*

"So… you do want to go and see your Daddy's new wife and child?"

"Yes, please."

I was unaware that Grandma's parents had sent their teenage daughter to America after she was raped by Russian soldiers during a program to be safe.

The following day, Aunt Jean said, "Maxine, don't be such a selfish child. Let Melvin color in your new book too."

I tore out a few pages and let him use my crayons. However, I became annoyed after he broke several of them. So, I took my book and crayons and went upstairs to play alone in the bedroom I shared with my mother.

***

Several days later, Uncle Larry packed my clothes in a large brown paper bag. He kissed me "goodbye" many, many times.

Grandma said, "Look how he's kissing her. It's like he thinks he'll never see her again."

Her words gave me hope Daddy was planning to keep me with him. I didn't like living here after he went away. But it would make me feel very sad not to see Larry any more. So, I waited at the front window until I saw Daddy's car park in front of the house. Then, I ran outside and Larry followed me. "Please, Daddy, can we take Uncle Larry with us?"

"No. Not this time, Maxine."

Larry kissed me goodbye again, and handed my packed bag to Daddy. He put it in the trunk. I climbed onto the back seat, stood up, and waved to Larry as we drove away.

I thought Daddy was going to his mother's house, or the tall brick house the blonde lady lived in., But that wasn't where we went.

He parked the car at the biggest drugstore I'd ever seen and took me inside.

He said, "Pick out presents to give to your new mother and sister."

I sobbed, "Daddy! I have no money."

He chuckled, "Silly child, I'm going to pay for them."

Daddy put the gifts in the trunk, and said, "Now we can go to my new home."

***

He drove to a small brick house I'd never before seen. He told me to knock on the door. I was surprised to see the woman who answered the door wasn't the blonde lady I'd met. "Hello," she said, "I'm Blanche, and this is my daughter, Selma."

15

I was shocked to see that my new sister wasn't a baby. She was bigger than Larry, and this lady had white in her hair just like my Grandma.

Blanche said to Selma," Take Maxine up to your room. She'll be sleeping in there while she's visiting with us."

Hearing her say this the hope of remaining in this house left me and I followed Selma. We passed by the living room before we climbed the stairs. In it I saw a tall live tree. It smelled very good to me.

As I went up the steps I saw Daddy come in and lay the wrapped presents we'd brought under the tree. I wondered why he'd did put them there.

***

Selma led me to her room. It was painted a pale rose pink, and had white curtains with ruffles that matched the bedspread. It took my breath away. It was the prettiest room I'd ever seen… *Selma has all this, and my daddy too.* I wished I was her.

CHAPTER 8

In the morning, Selma came in and showed me a paper doll book. "Which doll do you like?" she asked.

I pointed to one, and she cut that doll out for me, along with some paper clothes. Then, she showed me how to hang the paper doll's clothes on it. I had fun playing with Selma. I liked my new sister.

The following day she awakened me and said, "Santa Claus has been here!"

I followed her down the stairs. Then, I saw the tree in the living room was now decorated with pretty shiny colored balls, and lit up with colored beads of light all over it. What a wonderful sight to see. I sat down on the step to admire it.

Selma scolded, "What's the matter with you Maxine? Let's go get our presents."

I was surprised to hear I would be getting a gift today, and hurried after her.

"Selmoo", Blanche cooed from the living room. She grinned as she wheeled a red bicycle from behind the tree toward her happy daughter. "Look what Santa brought you."

Selma jumped up and down. "Oh, thank you Santa Claus! It's just what I wanted." I'd never heard of Santa Claus, and wondered who he was.

Blanche picked up another package. "Maxine, this is for you" she said.

I was thrilled that there was something for me. Quickly, I unwrapped the box. In it was a pretty dress I slipped it over my head immediately. "It fits me!"

It wasn't way too big on me like all my other clothes. I danced and twirled and the skirt flared out. "Oh, I love it! Thank you, Blanche."

I saw she shot Daddy a funny look, and said, "We'll open the rest of Santa's presents later. Let's go have breakfast now."

***

Selma's girl scout friends came to visit her. She introduced me as her little sister, Maxine. The uniformed girls had ridden their bicycles over to see Selma. They asked her to ride along with them.

"Mama, may I please go out and play with my friends?"

Blanche nodded, "Go with your friends, but be home by four o' clock." Then she turned and smiled at me. "Maxine, you come along with me into the kitchen, and we'll bake a cake." I liked to eat cake. This was going to be fun.

Blanche handed me a bag of flour to place on the table next to a book opened to a page with a picture of a cake on it. I watched as she read the recipe and measured each item into a big bowl. *Hmm. Grandma never reads a recipe book when she bakes a cake.*

"Maxine, stir this batter while I add the eggs and milk." We took turns mixing the batter. She let me rub the cake pans with butter. After that, Blanche sprinkled flour over the buttered pans. Grandma never did that either.

Blanche put the filled pans in the oven to bake. She didn't place a pan of water beneath them to help the cake rise. like Grandma did.

"Wasn't that fun?" Blanche asked me. I nodded.

"You're a shy child. Would you like me to read you a story?"

I nodded again and then followed her into the room with the pretty tree. I sat next to her. She smelled nice. Blanche read a story about someone called Santa Claus who brought toys, books, and clothes to <u>good</u> little girls and boys.

Hmm. So that's why I'm not on Santa's list. I'm a snitch. I sat sobbing, "I'll try to be a good girl, I promise."

Blanche hugged me. "You're a sweet child" she said.

CHAPTER 9

That night, I dreamt Uncle Larry and me were walking in a forest. We saw a house like the one in my "Hansel and Gretel" storybook. We walked to the front door and knocked. A green witch dressed in black wearing a pointed hat opened the door.

She grabbed me and shoved me into a cage. "I'm hungry" she said.

She ordered Larry to add wood to the fire under the oven. Then, the witch reached into the cage to take me out. "I'm going to eat you for my dinner," she said while opening the oven door.

Larry shouted, "No!" and he jumped into the open oven. The oven door slammed shut after him. I awoke screaming and scared.

Daddy and Blanche came running into the room. They turned on the lights.

"Did you have a bad dream?" Blanche asked.

I sobbed, "A witch ate my Larry!"

Daddy said, "It was only a bad dream, Maxine. Go back to sleep. Larry is all right."

I insisted. "No! No, I must go and see him."

Blanche suggested, "Can't we telephone the house? Let her speak to Larry on the phone."

Daddy said, "No. There's no telephone in that house. I'll have to take her back home in the morning."

***

Worried about Larry, I ran from the car after Daddy parked. I knocked on the front door. Aunt Jean opened it.

"What're you doing here?" she asked.

Daddy explained I'd had a nightmare and I insisted on coming home to see that Larry was all right. While they talked I was puzzled to see there were orange crates in the living room, and black cloths covered all the mirrors.

Jean said, "Larry is at the funeral parlor. I'm going there now." Daddy's face turned white.

I asked, "Can I go see Larry?"

Aunt Jean said, "Well, there's no time to find someone to leave you with…so you'll have to come along with me."

Daddy said, "I'll drive you both there."

We went to a house with black shutters. A man wearing a black hat, a black suit and a black tie was at the door. He gasped… "What? You've brought a little child here?"

"There was no time to leave her with anyone."

The man shook his head and led us down the hall to a closed door. I held onto Aunt Jean's hand. The man in black slid the door open. Inside the big room Grandma, my mother, Uncle Al, and Aunt Jean's husband, Joe were all seated. They were all crying.

I asked, "Where's Larry?"

"He's in the big box. Do you want to see him?" Grandma asked.

"Yes." I wondered why Larry was hiding in that box when everyone knew where he was hiding.

Grandma said to her other son, Al, "Lift up Maxine so she can see Larry in the box."

Uncle Al lifted me up and carried me to the platform. I was able to look down into the box. Larry wasn't in there. A small boy doll dressed in Larry's clothes was in the box. "Where's Uncle Larry?" I asked.

My mother said, "Silly child, he's in the box." I looked again. It was a small boy doll, but not my Uncle Larry. *Larry was much bigger than me. He was not little like this boy doll. Larry always smiled at me, and his hair hung over his forehead not like this boy doll.*

Grandma said, "Maxine should kiss him goodbye."

Uncle Al began to lower me to kiss that thing in the box. "No!" I shrieked.

Kicking and struggling, I managed to wriggle away from Uncle Al, and ran out of the room. In the hallway, my mother caught up with me and slapped my face.

"You made my mother cry. How dare you upset her!" she said, and raised her hand to slap me again.

However, the man in black who'd led me to the room caught hold of her hand, and said, "Madam, if you strike this child again I shall call the authorities."

He released her hand, and she lowered it and scurried back to the room looking frightened. The man handed me his folded handkerchief to wipe away my tears.

"You loved Larry very much," he said.

I nodded.

"Well, he's gone to live with the Lord."

"Why didn't Uncle Larry take me along with him?"

The man said, "It isn't your time yet. God has a plan for each of us."

I asked, "What's my plan?"

The man replied, "I don't know. You must go to school and learn to do many things. God will guide you to your plan."

Whimpering I said, "I don't go to school."

He smiled and asked, "How old are you?"

"Four and a half."

The man said, "Be patient. Wait a little longer. You'll go to school soon." I was comforted by what he'd said and stopped crying.

***

The others came out of the big room. We all walked to a long black car and got into it. It started to drizzle. No one had an umbrella. We were taken to a place where men buried the box. And a man with an umbrella said many words I didn't understand.

***

It rained harder as the car drove us back home. I watched quietly as the raindrops hit the window, and rolled down the glass until I fell asleep.

CHAPTER 10

In the morning, I came downstairs and saw the front door had been left open. Neighbors and friends brought in plates of food throughout the day. The family sat on the orange crates. I sat on the floor with Melvin. Grandma wept and sobbed day and night into her handkerchief.

Days later, strangers came into the house. They looked around, and selected something then handed Grandma money, and took away a piece of furniture, or some dishes.

One night, as my mother bathed me, she said, "We're moving to Brooklyn tomorrow."

I was worried and asked, "Will God know our new address?" I wanted Him to be able to find me and guide me.

"Silly child, He knows everything. You'd better be a good girl, or God will tell me if you're not." I was shocked to learn that God was a snitch. So, I would no longer trust Him with my secrets, or ask for His help.

**

In the morning mother reminded me, "Maxine, always call my mother your "Mama.' Do as you're told. Don't ask questions, and don't tell anyone what goes on inside our house." I asked, "Who are you?"

She laughed, "Silly child, I'm your sister, "Yetta."

"Oh, will you sleep in a pink bedroom?"

She gave me a startled look and said, "You're a strange child to ask me that question. Get dressed now."

The following day, two burly moving men arrived to carry out the remaining furniture, boxes of books, and household things. My mother had packed our clothes, and I watched the movers take apart my junior bed. Then they put the pieces in a big white truck, and drove away. I wondered if I would ever see my bed again?

"We're going to Brooklyn as soon as the taxi comes," Grandma screamed up the stairway. "Come down. The taxi is here."

A shiny yellow car with a light on its roof was parked in front of our house. Grandma said to the driver, "Go slow until we leave the neighborhood."

Her bulky body took up most of the backseat. My mother sat on the back seat too; with me on her lap. Uncle Al sat in the front seat holding a bunch of small packages. As we drove along the street. I waved goodbye to the boys on the corner.

Not one waved back. The taxi passed by the park, and the bare trees waved goodbye to us. Then the taxi drove over a bridge. Below, I saw big ships in the water. I believed we were moving to a far away land. My eyelids became heavy, and I soon fell asleep.

***

I awoke in my own little bed in a room I'd never seen. I heard a loud rattling sound and ran barefoot to the window. Standing on tiptoe I saw a long train on the elevated tracks in the distance screech to a stop. After that, I heard a "swooshing sound", and then the train moved on until it was out of sight.

My mother came to the doorway. "Breakfast is on the table. Remember not to call me your Mama. Listen to my mother, and call her 'Mama.' I'm going to work now," she said, and left.

I heard Grandma wail, "God why did you take away my little son?"

I went to the kitchen and climbed onto a chair. Grandma poured milk into my bowl. She asked, "Why did Larry have to die, and not you?"

Recalling what the funeral director had said to me, I answered, "It's not my time yet." She gave me a funny look, and stopped crying.

Wiping her eyes she said, "I need to go out to buy our food."

I asked, "Can I come?"

"No. You're not dressed. Brooklyn isn't like where we used to live. It's a jungle out there. You're safe in here. I love you. I'll be back soon." She walked out the door.

She'd lied to me before telling me about a monster in the closet. Was she telling me the truth, now, about Brooklyn? In my picture books jungles had no trains. I decided to dress quickly and try to catch up with my slow-moving grandmother.

I ran into the other room and pulled on my clothes. I ran to the door and grabbed the knob. It turned in my hand, but the door wouldn't open. What's wrong?

I'd always been able to open the doors where we used to live. I didn't want to be left alone in this strange place. I kicked and banged the door. "Let me out!"

It still wouldn't open. Frustrated and angry, I stomped to my bed and threw myself upon it, weeping.

***

When grandmother returned she gave me two jelly donuts for my supper. After it got very dark, then my mother came home from work.

She asked her mother, "Was Maxine a good girl today?" She held a wooden coat hanger in her hand while she spoke.

Grandma answered, "The neighbors complained she makes too much noise."

"Ma, if Maxine made you unhappy, I'm sorry."

After that, she turned to face me and said, "If I hear you've been bad, or made my mother unhappy, I'll hit you with this hanger. Understand?"

I believed she was mad at me for causing her life to be difficult now. I sensed I didn't dare to complain that Grandma had only given me donuts for my dinner, and left me alone all day. My mother didn't care if I wasn't happy.

CHAPTER 11

The following morning, I dressed before I went into the kitchen for breakfast. Grandma had put the Rice Krispies, and milk in my bowl, but they were no longer snapping and crackling.

"I don't want it."

Grandma snarled and said, "Eat it! Children in China are starving. Don't waste food. I'll make you oatmeal tomorrow." I did as she told me to and ate it.

"Mama, I'm dressed. Can I go with you today?"

"No. It's a jungle out there. I love you. In here I know you're safe. I don't want you to get hurt."

***

After she left, I explored the kitchen looking for something to play with and found crawling cockroaches. *Ugh.* Upset, I ran to my mother's bedroom.

I was able to open that door. Her bedroom was painted the same pink color as the false-teeth Grandma left in the glass at night on the bathroom sink. *Ugh.* I climbed onto her bed. A train rattled past on its way to the station.

I lay there and wished things would go back to as they were before I'd asked her why she didn't paint her fingernails. *Sigh.*

***

Recalling Daddy had stopped being angry with me, I was hoping my mother would like me again too. *I wanted my Mama to want me.* I started crying and left her bedroom.

I felt safer in my own little bed. I pulled the blanket over my head and prayed, *Please God make mother like me again*

***.

Each night when mother came home she would ask, "Was Maxine a good girl?"

I knew I better be good, or she'd hit me with the wooden hanger. I stopped asking Grandma to let me go out with her, and didn't dare to bang on the front door any more.

***

I was lonely. By standing on a kitchen chair, I was able to look through the closed window to the windows across the driveway. They had curtains on them. Day after day I waited and watched, but no one ever came to look out.

Often, I would make believe someone had come to the window, and I would talk to the imaginary person, or animal.

***

One day, I heard music coming from the outside. With great difficulty I managed to open the kitchen window wide enough to stick my head out. There was no green jungle down there. It was just pavement that I saw.

A man was standing in the driveway making the wonderful music. Several boys and girls were listening to the fiddler play. I knew the song he was playing, and sang the words to it.

He looked up and waved to me. "Shana maedel," he said, and waved his bow. Then, he played a song just for me. More windows opened. Coins were thrown down to him. The fiddler bowed, gathered them, and left. All the children followed him. I wanted to follow him too.

I forgot that I wasn't able to open the front door. I tried, but it still would not open when I turned the knob. I slumped down to the floor and cried, and I fell asleep.

***

I was awakened by a clicking noise high above my head. Looking up, I saw a small knob turning to and fro, and heard Grandma muttering as she tried to open the door to come inside.

I realized my body was holding the door shut, and keeping her from entering. I ran into the other room. Grandma entered the kitchen.

A-ha! To open the door I will need to turn the little knob on the door.

***

Next day, after Grandma left, I dragged a chair to the door, and stood on it to reach the small knob. It turned easily. I dragged the chair away, and was able to open the door. I was free!

I hurried down the stairway to the front door, and the street. I discovered I lived in a two-story building as I went down the stairs. I opened the door to the street, and saw this place was different from where we'd once lived… No trees lined the street. No people were passing by.

Statues of stone lions sat atop the concrete front steps. This house was next to an empty lot littered with cans and empty bottles. Across the large wide busy street was a tall brick building. A tall locked gate surrounded it.

This place was different, but it wasn't a jungle. Lots of cars whizzed by. I wanted to run about the sidewalk, but decided to sit on the stone lion and consider what I should do next carefully. *If I fell and got hurt, Grandma would say, "See! I was right to keep you safe inside.'*»

As I sat thinking, a lady with packages in her arms came toward me. I jumped up to open and hold the door for her.

"What a sweet child you are. Are you visiting someone in the building?"

I shook my head. "No. I live upstairs."

I was surprised to hear the lady say, "Why, you're no monster." *Hmm. I wonder who told her that?*

"I'm Mrs. Rosen. My sister lives in a building where quite a few teen-aged girls want to become babysitters live. But, there're no small children to practice

with. Would you like to come with me, and play with
   them?" I nodded my head.

She said, "While I put away my groceries, you go up and ask your Mama if you may come along with me when I go to help my sister."

I climbed the stairs "to ask." I made believe "Mama" had said, "Maxine, you may go, but come home by four o'clock." Mrs. Rosen believed my lie. "Oh, we'll be back long before that time."

***

The nice lady held my hand as we walked along the sidewalk. We crossed a street and went to a group of buildings. Teenaged girls were standing in the courtyard.

"Hi, girls. This is Maxine. She wants to play with you."

The teenagers all smiled at me, and we joined hands and sang, "Ring around the Rosie." Next, we played the motorboat game.

Oh goodie. I was having a lot of fun.

They showed me how to play "Potsie, "Statues", "May I?" and a game named "Steps."

***

Mrs. Rosen came back, and she walked me home. I asked, "Can we go tomorrow?"

She smiled and said, "I'm glad you had a good time. Knock on my door after you have breakfast."

The following day, as soon as Grandma left the apartment, I went to see Mrs. Rosen. I saw that there was an apartment in the rear, and in the front of the building. Mrs. Rosen lived in the rear apartment below us.

As we walked down the street, she stopped to speak to a few of the neighbors. She introduced me, and like Shirley Temple did in "Heidi," a movie film Daddy had taken me to see, I curtsied.

The ladies all smiled, and patted me on the head, and said, "Sweet child."

When asked questions by the neighbors, I would mumble in a soft voice until they stopped asking me questions. Keeping secrets was a heavy burden for a blabbermouth like me.

CHAPTER 12

"**M**ama" didn't catch on that I knew how to get out of the apartment, until one day, a neighbor gave her a no-longer-used doll to give to me. Puzzled, she returned to the locked apartment, "This is for you, Houdini," she said, and handed me the doll.

That night, she said, "Oy, Yetta, I was so upset today to find Maxine was missing. The lady in the apartment below us took her for a walk without asking my permission."

My mother's face got red, and she said, "I'm going to tell off that brazen woman," and hurried downstairs. Overhearing her yelling at my friend I felt like crying.

In the morning, I knocked on Mrs. Rosen's door. She opened it, and on seeing me, said, "You are a monster." After that, she slammed the door in my face.

I felt really bad she would no longer take me with her. It had been fun playing with the big girls.

***

One day, as I sat on the stone lion, Aunt Jean and my cousin, Melvin, came up to me, "Hello Maxine. We're going to live here now, too. A lady moved away, and we've rented her apartment."

I asked, "Who moved out?"

She said, "I don't know her name, but it's the apartment right below where my mother lives." That's how I learned Mrs. Rosen had moved away.

***

One morning, "Mama," Yetta, and me were seated at the kitchen table when I saw my mother open her purse and take out some money. "Ma, I hired Kurt

Schultz, the neighbor you recommended to install the venetian blinds. He gave me a good price. He's coming here this morning. Give him this cash when he finishes the job."

Grandma put the money in the pocket of her dress, and my mother left for work.

Before I finished my breakfast, a man came to the apartment door carrying several boxes. Curiously, I followed him from window to window watching him install the blinds. He finished hanging all the blinds. "I want to be paid," he said.

"Mama has your money," I told him and went to find her. That's when I discovered she'd gone. Grandma had left me alone in the apartment with this strange man.

The man said, "Oh, I get it. She left you here as my pay for this job."

I responded "No. "Mama" has money for you in her pocket."

He grasped my hand and dragged me along with him to my mother's bedroom while I kept insisting, "'Mama' is coming back. She has the money for you."

The man didn't pay any attention to what I was saying. He picked me up and placed me on the bed. I was bewildered when he pulled off my panties, and began to lick me between my legs.

"Doesn't that feel good?" he asked.

I didn't believe he cared how I felt. "I have to make a wee-wee," I told him, and he let me slip off the bed.

Then, I ran to the bathroom and locked the door.

He came after me and shouted: "Open up!"

I was frightened yet thought my *Grandma will be home soon to pay him. I won't open the door.* As it started to get dark, I wondered, *Where is she?*

From the driveway, I heard a woman's voice shout, "Kurt. Dinner is on the table. Come home."

I hoped he'd left yet was afraid to unlock the door. When I heard the clatter of pots I figured "Mama" had finally gotten home, and I came out of the locked bathroom.

Sobbing, I faced her, "Where did you go?"

She didn't answer my question, but asked, "What happened?"

I sobbed, "Nothing." Angrily I shouted, "You didn't pay him! You're bad. You have money in your pocket that my mother gave you to pay him."

"Stop crying, Maxine. If you don't tell Yetta, I have it, I won't ever tell her I'm unhappy with you anymore."

Hmm. Not getting hit with the wooden hanger was more important to me than telling my mother what happened here today. So, I nodded, and dried my eyes.

CHAPTER 13

One afternoon, seated on the stone lion, I saw a group of boys and girls coming out of the red building across the street, and walk through the open gates. Some of the children were greeted by women. The other boys and girls walked to the corner where a woman led them across the street after the cars had stopped moving.

One of these children was my cousin, Melvin. I asked him, "What did you do inside that place?"

Proudly he said, "I go to school. I'm in first grade."

He went inside the house, and I followed him. He opened his schoolbag and showed his mother what he did today.

"When do I go to school, Aunt Jean?"

She said, "You must be registered before you can go to school."

I hurried upstairs. "'Mama" you need to register me for school."

She said, "I didn't go to school. You're smart like me. You don't need to go to school either."

At supper, I told my mother, "Melvin goes to school. I want to go to school."

She said, "Ma, register Maxine at the school tomorrow." Grandma responded, "Why does a girl need to go to school?"

Yetta replied, "It's the law, Ma. Maxine must learn to read and write."

***

The following day, my grandmother held my hand and we crossed the street. We entered the school. It was a very different place than any building I'd ever been in.

"Mama" took me to a room where there was a lady was behind the counter. Grandma explained why we was there. The lady handed her papers, and told her to fill them out, but "Mama" said, "Oh, I forgot my eyeglasses. Please, will you fill them out for me?"

I knew Grandma didn't have eyeglasses. She was not telling the truth to the lady.

When the paperwork was finished, the lady took my hand and led us to the schoolyard. "Maxine, when you come here tomorrow morning you'll stand behind this yellow line with the letter "K" on it."

Then, she pointed to the open gates, and said to my "Mama", "That's where you may pick up your child at the end of the school day." Grandma said: "Goodbye, Maxine," and left us.

The lady brought me back inside, and led me to a Kindergarten classroom. She introduced me to Mrs. Lynch, my kindergarten teacher.

I was glad to see the boys and girls in the room were my size. I looked forward to playing games with them.

***

When school was over, Grandma was not at the gate waiting for me. I went to the corner and was led across the street. I walked to my house. She was not inside waiting for me. So, I showed my doll what I had done in school today.

Next morning, Melvin didn't wait for me to go to school with him. I walked to the corner, and crossed the street with the other children. When I returned home, I was very upset to find that my bed was no longer there. It was gone.

"'Mama,' where's my bed?"

"I sold it. You're a big girl now. You go to school. I gotten dollars for the bed."

"Where will I sleep?"

"Your mother has a double bed. Sleep with her."

CHAPTER 14

On Saturdays, mother didn't work, and there was no school. Seated on the stoop, I was playing with my doll one Saturday morning when Melvin showed up with a friend.

He said, "Eugene and me are going to beat you up."

I took my doll and ran inside to my apartment. My mother asked, "Why did you come upstairs on such a nice day?"

"Melvin and his friend want to hit me."

Mama accompanied me downstairs. I thought she would scold Melvin. To my surprise, she pushed me out the door, and stood behind it holding it shut against my entering.

"Let me in! They're going to hit me." She wouldn't open the door. I was furious she wanted me to get hit. I saw red and went down the stairs to fight the boys while I wept.

I kicked and hit them until they ran away. Then, still sobbing, I went upstairs.

My mother said, "See. You must learn to fight your own battles, Maxine."

What I'd learned was that no one here cared what happens to me. I knew that they missed Larry because he wasn't here. I thought, *If I wasn't here no more they'd miss me too, and be sorry."*

So, I took a box of animal crackers from the cupboard, and ran away. I went to the corner. No one was there to help me cross the busy street. I wasn't allowed to cross the street by myself. So, I sat down on the curb and told each animal in the box before I ate it, "When I go back home they'll be glad to see me."

After the cookies were all eaten, I decided I'd been away long enough for them to miss me. *They'll be sorry now they didn't care about me.*

I returned home, but I saw that no one had even noticed I'd been gone.

Upset, I threw myself on the bed and cried.

My mother asked, "What's the matter, Maxine?"

"Nobody here cares about me!"

"I care about you."

I wept. "No. You don't!"

After that, she told me about the man in the long black car in Richmond Hill. "He's a very rich man. He owns the Green Giant factories. He asked me to let you be his little girl, but I told him, "No."

Sobbing, I asked, "If he wanted me, why didn't you give me to him?"
"What would the neighbors have thought if I did that?"

***

I wished my father had taken me with him when he'd left. I hoped one day he would come, and take me away to live in his new home.

***

A few months later Grandma said, "Maxine, you go to school. Did you learn to read and write?" I nodded, and she said, "Show me."

I took out my pad and drew the letters that I'd learned. I opened my reader and pointed to each word, explaining how to pronounce it. It was fun being a teacher.

She was unable to follow all my instructions, and became impatient with herself, saying, "Humph. I'm smart enough. I don't need to read."

She went outside to be with her friends who invited her to have coffee and cake.

***

On Friday nights, Grandma would place a lace cloth on her head, and light Sabbath candles. She would raise her hands, bow her head, and mutter the Sabbath prayer. I wanted to learn her prayer too.

"'Mama' please teach me to say your prayer."

I was surprised when she scolded me for making fun of her. I'd only wanted to learn the Sabbath prayer to God. It never occurred to me Grandma had never learned all the words of the prayer properly. It was her secret. She had been forced to flee Russia as a small child, and was only imitating what she saw her mother do.

Saying the Friday night prayer, fasting, and Passover were the only Jewish traditions Grandma recalled.

CHAPTER 15

No one was ever in the apartment to greet me when I came home from school from start to finish. One day, I accepted an invitation from my classmate, Elaine Hoffman, to go home with her.

Mrs. Hoffman gave us milk and cookies. We did our homework together. I saw how a "real mother" treats her daughter.

My mother was never at home for me. *Sigh*. I thought it was my fault she needed to work, and date men. I didn't judge her to be an uncaring mother.

I liked Elaine, and envied her mother. However, it felt worse to me being with her in her house than it did being alone in my empty apartment.

Walking home from her house, I saw a "Help Wanted" sign in the window of the bicycle store on a street corner. I went in and asked for the job. No one else had applied. The owner wanted to work uninterrupted assembling new bikes for Christmas in the rear of his store.

He hired me to check his bicycles out and in to people who wanted to rent them, until he could hire a more qualified person to do this job. I removed the sign from the window, and hid it.

No one asked me about what I did after school, and I didn't tell anyone. Grandma kept Yetta's money. I knew she would take my money if she saw it. So, I kept my pay in my desk at school.

One day, the teacher said, "Children, when you get older and earn money, don't join a Christmas Club at the bank. It upsets me to see people don't understand by having a savings account, they could be earning interest on their money."

Aha! The bank is a better place to keep my money than my desk. After school I hurried to the bank to open a savings account.

***

I was told I was too young to open an account. "Oh, it's not for me," I lied. "It's for my mother. She's sick and can't walk here." The lady at the desk believed me, and handed me the papers to be filled out by my mother to open an account.

Next day, I returned with my money, and the forms filled out. I kept the passbook in my desk. I liked the idea of my money now earning money.

***

The teacher passed out report cards for our parents to sign. I was surprised to hear Elaine and several other children groaning about the grades they had received.

Elaine said, "Mommy won't like these grades. She'll stop my allowance." "Daddy will whip me when he sees my card," one boy said.

I was secretly pleased to hear the concerns of my classmates. This was something I liked about having Yetta as my mother. She signed my card and never commented on my grades.

What's an allowance? I wondered.

***

We learned President Abraham Lincoln had freed the slaves, and would always be remembered for that. After class, I spoke to my teacher. "I understand slavery is a bad thing, but what is it?"

She said, "Slavery is when you work but receive no pay for doing it."

I do the shopping for Aunt Jean. Melvin won't do it for her. She must think I'm her slave.

When I got home, Jean asked me to go shopping for her. I took the money she gave me and went to the store. I bought the items that she needed to make her dinner.

I thought, *This is Friday night. Grandma will make me a burnt burger for dinner. I'll have to break it apart and add it to the mashed potatoes so I can eat it. Ugh.*

Meanwhile, Melvin will have this good food to eat tonight. *I do things for Jean and she never invites me to eat with her family. It's not fair. I'm not her slave.*

I used the change the grocer gave me to buy my dinner: a hot dog on a bun, and an ice-cream cone. Then I delivered the groceries to my auntie.

"Oh, thank you," she said. "You're such a good girl. Er-r. Maxine, where's my change?" I handed her the few coins that were left in my pocket.

"Where's the rest of it?"

I told her what I'd done with the change. She said, "That was my money."

I said, "No. It was my pay. I'm not your slave."

My Aunt opened and closed her mouth, but couldn't find the right words. "When your mother comes home I'm going to tell what you did!"

Later, Jean did complain to Yetta who laughed, "My daughter is smart enough to go to college."

Aunt Jean stopped asking me to do her shopping, or switch on the lights for her on Friday at sundown. I resented her for asking me to turn on the lights after I learned from a friend Jews weren't supposed to switch on electric lights when the sun went down on Friday nights. Aunt Jean had used my ignorance to cause me to sin.

CHAPTER 16

I didn't like being the only girl in my class who wore long braids. One day, Wallace La Peters, the boy who sat behind me, dipped one of my pigtails into the inkwell on his desk. Blue ink spattered over the back of my white blouse during the day.

I was unaware of it. When I returned home "Grandma scolded me for being careless. She complained about it to my mother who realized what must've happened. "It's not Maxine's fault. Ma, I won't hit her."

I asked my mother if she would get my knee length hair cut short and styled like the other girls in my class.

Grandma said, "Yetta, if you cut off Maxine's braids she'll look older. Do you want the men you date to think you're old?" So, my mother cut the blue ends from my hair, and pinned the braids across the top my head.

***

Mama had bought a box of white shirts for me to wear to school, and the following day I wore another one to class.

One of the girls asked, "How did your Mama get the ink off your blouse?"

"She didn't get it off. This is another blouse."

"Oh-h. We all thought you always wore the same blouse to school every day."

"No. I have a box full of them."

After that incident, I was allowed to jump rope with the girls, and no longer had to be "the steady ender"; one of the two girls who twirl the rope so others can jump.

World War 2 was being waged by the United States against the Nazis. On Auditorium Day, the Principal announced the Air Force needed hair eighteen inches or longer, and would pay for the haircut of any girl who qualified.

As soon as school ended, I hurried to the principal's office to do my patriotic duty. I was surprised to see Melvin and Aunt Jean seated on a bench waiting outside his office aid, "You can go in before us, Maxine," she said, and I did.

With the voucher in my hand I hurried to the beauty shop, a few doors down from the bicycle store. I was eager to do my patriotic duty.

The hair stylist told me to sit in his special chair. He cut my hair and swept it from all corners of the store into a special canvas bag. After that, he styled a short haircut for me.

I was delighted to see my reflection in the mirror. Yes, I did look older. I knew Yetta and Grandma were going to be angry. As I walked home, I admired my new hairdo in each store front window I passed.

My head felt as if a great weight had been lifted from it. *Ha! It's off. What can they do about it?* My mother will no longer be combing and re-braiding my hair Saturday mornings. I won't need to sit and be afraid to cry out, and upset her any more. *I'm glad I did it.*

When I entered the apartment Grandma shrieked. "What have you done to your hair?"

"I had a haircut."

"I can see that. Just you wait 'til your mother comes home. She's going to give it to you. What else bad did you do? Jean told me you went in to see the principal.

"Nothing" I replied. "Was Melvin bad? Is that why they were sitting outside Mr. Rubel's office?"

"Never you mind. It's none of your business! I hear your mother coming up the steps." She hurried to open the door. "Look at what your daughter has done."

"Maxine, who gave you the money to get a haircut?"

"The principal gave me a voucher. The United States Air Force needed my hair for the Norden bombsight. Mr. Rubel thanked me for doing this

"Patriotic service to help my country."

"Oh," she gasped and turned proudly to her mother, "See Ma? Maxine has contributed to the war effort. We can't fault her for that."

"Why was Melvin at the Principal's office with Aunt Jean?" I asked. I didn't wait to hear the answer. I left the room before Grandma answered the question.

From the bedroom I overheard my mother exclaim, "Melvin's so dumb they're leaving him back?"

CHAPTER 17

Mrs. Richardson, my third-grade teacher, gave me an envelope to give to my mother. I gave it to her without looking at the papers inside.

On Saturday, I was surprised to see Daddy arrive at the apartment. *He usually came to see us at the start of each month. Why was here today?*

My mother told me they had an important matter to discuss. "Go play outside."

When I returned, I asked, "Where's Daddy?"

"Your father had to go back to his "engineering" job at the department store on Pitkin Avenue." I was disappointed he hadn't stayed to spend some time with me, or even say goodbye.

***

On the last day of class before summer vacation, Mrs. Richardson gave out our report cards. I was unhappy to hear Carole Broder brag she was being skipped a grade. I considered myself to be as smart as she was. So, I stayed after class to speak with the teacher.

"My grades were as good as Carole's. Why wasn't I skipped too?"

Mrs. Richardson surprised me when she said, "I agree with you, Maxine. I sent papers home that would allow you to be skipped, but your parents refused to sign them."

Oh? I'm smart. Why didn't Daddy and Yetta want me to be skipped? From now on I'll read anything sent home about me, and I'll do the signing when I think it's right for me.

***

At the bicycle shop, I asked Roberto if he wanted me to come to work earlier now that school was out. He looked me over from head to toe before he said, "You're looking good to me kiddo. How would you like me to buy you a new dress?"

"Why would you want to do that?"

"You'll be my girlfriend." He panted. "Go to the back of the store. I'll show you how much fun we can have together."

"No thank you," I said, and hurried out of there. I didn't want to be Roberto's girlfriend. I was sorry to no longer have a job, and I went home.

At the apartment, Aunt Jean was cleaning an ugly cut on Grandma's leg.

"What happened?" I asked.

"She was collecting discarded metal from an empty lot. She wanted to help the war effort too. A jagged piece of metal cut her on the leg."

When my mother came home she sent me to fetch the doctor who lived around the corner. I told him what happened. He knew Grandma, and closed his office to come home with me.

While I was doing my homework on the kitchen table, I overheard him tell Yetta and Jean their mother was a diabetic. He'd tried to convince her to take insulin, and go on a diet. However, she refused to follow his advice.

"I'll put sulfur powder on her wound. If it doesn't heal, or it becomes discolored, she'll have to go to the hospital. In the meantime, she needs to keep her leg elevated."

Grandma's friends visited until they grew weary of hearing her constant complaining. I felt sorry for her. I knew what it was like to be alone all day.

After school, I did the shopping. Each night, Grandma complained to her daughters while I sat and did my homework at the kitchen table.

One evening, my mother came home with a radio she'd bought to keep her mother company. When I came home for lunch the next day, Grandma told me about "Ma Perkins" and "Helen Trent" radio programs.

They became her favorite soap operas. She commiserated with "Ma" whose children weren't doing well in their lives either.

CHAPTER 18

On Saturdays, "Mama" let me to listen to "Let's Pretend." The cast performed the fairy tales I'd read, and I loved listening to them.

One day after listening to the program, I noticed that Grandma's injury hadn't healed, and she had purple streaks running down her leg.

I went downstairs to tell Aunt Jean. She didn't believe me, and came up to investigate. Convinced, she went for the doctor. He examined Grandma and decided she had to go to the hospital.

While Grandma was hospitalized, I found a number of radio programs that were of interest to me. I listened to them while I did the housework, or my homework.

One evening, mom came home after visiting her mother. She saw me listening to the radio, and turned it off. She said, "I bought this radio for my mother, and not you."

"It's lonely here. I do the housework. I don't get an allowance. I feel entitled to listen to the radio."

"I work and pay the bills with Grandma. I can't afford to pay you. I put food in your mouth and clothes on your back. Your father gives me no more money for your support. It's time you earned your keep."

She lit a cigarette and continued, "They cut off your grandmother's leg. She's a diabetic and needs insulin shots. Jean won't do it.

The nurse is going to teach you how to give her injections when we bring her home tomorrow."

"I don't want to stick her with a needle either."

"Never you mind what you want. It must be done, Maxine, and you'll do it." The next day a nurse brought Grandma home along with her artificial leg. My mother pointed to me and told the nurse to teach me how to give her mother injections.

The nurse gasped. "You want the little girl to administer the injections to your mother?"

"Yes. She's eleven years old, and a smart kid."

I learned to give Grandma a daily shot before I left for school. I knew she needed the insulin yet I resented having to be the one to give her the injections.

Grandma joked with her visitors, "Look at me. Don't I look good for a person with one leg in the grave?" I admired her attitude.

***

CHAPTER 19

Each time Daddy came he promised me that one day he would take me to live with him. Then, he stopped coming. I overheard my mother complain to Grandma he was no longer giving her any money for child support.

Had he stopped loving me? I was tired of hearing his assurances telling me to wait a little longer. He'd had more than enough time to arrange for me to come live with him. I was unhappy living with Mama and Grandma. I hated it, and wanted to leave this place. I decided to visit my father to remind him he'd promised to take me away from here.

I took the bus to Pitkin Avenue. I found the large department store he worked for, and hoped my Dad was still working there, I'd told my mother I would ask him for the child support money.

***

I told the man wearing a blue suit behind the counter, "Sydney Reichard is the engineer here. He's my father, and I need to see him."

The man led me to where my father was working along with two other men dressed in gray uniforms. I was surprised to see Daddy wore a grey uniform. *He's not an engineer. He's a janitor.*

On seeing me, Daddy's eyebrows shot up. "Maxine, what are you doing here?"

"Mother told me you forgot to give her my money."

Immediately, he reached into his trouser pocket and withdrew a wad of bills. He handed me half of his cash. *Oh, Daddy still loves me.*

He took a roll of Life Saver mints from his shirt pocket and offered me one. I smiled and put it in my pocket. Daddy is my real-life lifesaver. I was hoping I was going to live with him.

Dad introduced me to his coworkers. "This is my daughter, Maxine." *Ah, my father is proud of me.*

"Daddy, I have something important to ask you."

"Sure, Maxine. I'll take you outside. We can talk there."

***

He took my arm and ushered me to the front of the building. There, he grabbed back the cash he'd given to me and snarled, "Don't you ever come here again and embarrass me in front of my co-workers."

Sobbing, I said, "Daddy, I can't stand living there anymore. When are you going to take me to live with you?"

"Maxine, it's my wife's house. She doesn't want you to live with us. You may not understand this now, but in life you've got to make your own bed. I've made mine. It's a good one. It's time for you to make yours. You have to stay with your mother. I need to go back to work. I can't afford to lose this job.

Goodbye, Darling."

Although I stood on a firm sidewalk, I wobbled as if the earth beneath me were giving way. Hope of escaping Grandma's home was gone.

I leaned against the building. My father had been leading me on all this time to believe something he knew was never going to happen. I felt betrayed…I despised him. *Men cheat and lie.*

Although I'd heard, "The truth will set you free… hearing the truth from my father felt as though a key had turned locking the cell of my imprisonment. I was very upset and slowly walked toward home.

***

As I was passing Lincoln Terrace Park, a medium-sized white terrier with large brown spots came up to me. His fur was caked with dirt. He wagged his tail and looked at me with his bright brown eyes. I pitied him. *He must be lost, or abandoned.*

"No one cares about you either," I said. "I bet you're hungry." I gave him the mint in my pocket. He ate it, and followed me home.

Grandma was asleep in the front bedroom when we came in. I led the dog to the bathroom and bathed him in the tub. I wanted to clean him up before I showed him to "Mama" and Yetta.

CHAPTER 20

I introduced the dog to Grandma. She petted him and put him on her lap. When my mother came home, I said, "'Mama' needs company. Can we keep this dog as her pet?"

My mother sighed and said, "Another mouth to feed?" "A dog is good protection against burglars," Grandma said.

I was glad she liked the idea of having a dog in the apartment to keep her company.

"I'll walk Skippy before I go to school, and when I come home. Please, can we keep him?"

She said, "Well, let's try it out for a few days. Ma, what do you want to call the dog?"

"Skippy is a good enough name for a dog."

***

It felt good to come home and be greeted by Skippy; wagging his tail. I loved him. He licked my face and was always happy to see me. We're kindred spirits. I walked him in the empty lot next door.

***

Grandma had been told by the nurse to practice walking each day with her artificial leg. She claimed that the leg was too heavy and uncomfortable. She also refused to walk with her crutches. She remained in her bed, and used a bedpan to go to the bathroom. I had to empty it, wash it, and return it to her.

***

One day, Grandma asked me to bring her a bar of butter. She smeared it on her leg stump, and then encouraged Skippy to lick it off. She seemed to enjoy it, and so did the dog.

***

In class my seatmate said, "I have something to show you. Meet me in the bathroom." I went to meet her there.

In the stall she pulled down her panties to show me a pad with blood on it. "Oh Marlene, I'm so sorry you're sick."

"I'm not sick. I'm a woman now. I'm menstruating. My mother bought me a bunch of daisies to celebrate the day I became a woman. I can grow a baby now when I get married."

"Wow. That's good news."

***

Several days later, I awoke and went to urinate, and wiped myself. I was surprised to see blood on the tissues when I flushed the toilet. Then, I realized I'd begun to menstruate too.

Excited, I walked over to my mother before she left for work to tell her I was now menstruating. I expected her to congratulate me for becoming a woman. Perhaps she'd buy me a flower. I told mama, and to my surprise she slapped my face.

Bewildered, I asked, "Why did you hit me?"

"It's what I'm supposed to do. I don't know the reason. My mother did it to me, and her mother did it to her."

I thought it was a stupid custom, and determined if I ever had a daughter I would buy her flowers, and not slap her face.

***

Grandma developed bedsores. Her daughters searched to find a wheelchair large enough to accommodate their fat mother. They finally found a wooden, over-sized wheelchair, but it couldn't pass through any of the doorways. So, Grandma was restricted to the kitchen whenever she sat on it.

She needed the help of Uncle Joe to get into, and out of the bed to the chair. Grandma preferred the chair to the bed, and she often slept in the chair.

It was unpleasant for me to live in Grandma's apartment with my mother. I thought about getting a full-time job and moving out. *Who needs to finish school? I know how to read, write, and do arithmetic. What more is there for me to learn?*

I became twelve, but I was still too young to get my working papers. I dreamt about getting a job where I'd earn promotions. Then, I could hire my classmates after they had finished school.

In my junior high-school economics class the teacher told us about the stock market. Suddenly, it seemed as if a light had been turned on inside my head. The teacher had opened a window to let me see something new in the adult world. I'd no idea such a thing existed. *Aha! There's more for me to learn here. I'd better stay in school.*

After class, I asked my teacher, "How does one get into the stock market?" He said, "You buy a full coverage newspaper, and pick the stock you want. After that, you call a broker to purchase the stock for you, and then you send him the money to pay for it."

After I'd quit my job with Roberto, I got a job taking care of a neighbor's over-active child. She used my services a lot. I put the money I earned into my bank account.

On Sunday, I eagerly used my babysitting money to buy the New York Times. It had more sections in it than any other newspaper. I turned to the business part and found pages and pages of listed stocks. How do I know which one to pick? *Hmm. This is another good reason for me to stay in school.* Maybe I'll be taught how to pick a stock for me to buy.

***

At home, I continued to scrub the twenty-five-foot linoleum kitchen, and bathroom floors on my knees, polish the furniture, look after Grandma, and do the shopping.

One day, in the grocery store, I lifted up a large can off the shelf and found to my surprise it didn't feel as heavy as other cans the same size. *Why isn't this can as heavy as the other cans?*

I read the can's label and learned it was made of aluminum. *Aha! Other customers will want to buy their food in these lighter cans also. I was certain this company would do well. If it's on the stock market I'll put all my money into this can manufacturer.*

The following day, I used the phone book to find a stockbroker. I called and said, "I have three hundred dollars to invest in the Aluminum Can Company of America."

At the bank I gave instructions to send a check for that amount to the broker. Seventy-five cents remained in my account. I was elated to be the owner of shares in a good growing company. After that I returned to the house.

CHAPTER 21

I opened the front door of the four-family building and heard an eerie voice echoing through the tiled hallway. Approaching the staircase, I recognized the muttered words…, "God bless you."

I edged up the steps and saw my grandmother seated in her wheelchair, blocking the kitchen doorway, nodding her head and chanting. Her skin was sallow from lack of sunshine. She had dark circles beneath her eyes.

I said, "Please move your chair away from the door." It took several requests before she finally responded, and rolled her chair away.

I asked, "Where's Skippy? I'm ready to walk him before I do my homework."

She said, "The door was open. He must've run out."

I hurried outside to find my dog. I searched the neighborhood calling, "Skippy!" I couldn't find him.

I returned home… very sad and upset that the dog was gone.

Grandma's chanting seemed very strange to me, and I told my mother about it when she came home.

She said, "Mind your own business. My mother is doing the best she can. It's hard for her to be cooped up here all day."

I do all I can to help her mother yet she scolds me. Tears sprang to my eyes. She didn't appreciate my efforts or concern for her mother. I hurried to the bathroom where I'd be alone, and not be questioned as to why I was weeping.

CHAPTER 22

One evening while I did my homework, Grandma asked me to go downstairs to find out when Uncle Joe was coming up to kill her. I stared at her in disbelief. *She's crazy.*

She badgered me with the same request continued for several nights. Finally, I went down to Jean's apartment and told her. She was skeptical but came upstairs with me anyway.

"Ma, why are you afraid of my husband?"

I was amazed when Grandma said, "What nonsense are you talking? I'm not afraid of Joe. Whoever told you such a silly thing? The girl must be crazy."

I was bewildered and flabbergasted. "Don't you ever ask me to go downstairs for you again," I said, and ran to the rear bedroom. *Why had the old lady bothered to outfox me? What plan did she have working in her head for me?*

I overheard Jean tell her mother to rap on the radiator if she needed her help.

Puzzled and feeling wary of Grandma, I stayed away from her as much as possible. I did my homework in the public library, and when I babysat.

***

At school, I filled out and signed the proper forms to eat a free lunch in the school cafeteria. However, I had to go home to sleep and be there in the morning to give Grandma her insulin.

I overheard my mother tell Grandma she was going to visit a friend in Atlantic City for the weekend. So, I accepted babysitting jobs for Thursday, Friday and Saturday evening in order to stay away from home.

***

Early Sunday morning something awakened me. I looked around the room and saw Grandma's reflection at the kitchen doorway in the mirror over the bedroom dresser. Curious, I watched as she wrapped twine around the left arm of her chair. Then, she slid a long kitchen knife under the twine. After that she covered it with a dishtowel.

Hmm. Is she doing that because she believes Joe will try to hurt her? She'll be ready now to defend herself if need be. I yawned, and went back to sleep. I spent Sunday at the public library.

***

Monday morning, I awoke in our cold apartment, and took my clothes from the top of the radiator. I'd placed them there the night before to have them warm up for me in the morning. I left the bedroom and walked toward the bathroom to wash up.

Grandma was seated in her wheelchair in the kitchen doorway blocking my way to the bathroom.

"Please move your chair and let me pass."

She answered, "No. Climb over me,"

I knew about the knife, and was suspicious of her strange request. I didn't trust her. I was afraid she might want to hurt me.

I screamed, "I'll be late for school if you don't roll your chair back."

She must have realized then I wouldn't climb over her. She moved back a foot. It was enough for me to squeeze through and run into the bathroom before she could come toward me with the knife in her hand.

I'd escaped injury, but my heart was beating wildly. *I've done everything I can to help her. Why does she want to hurt me? Is she crazy?*

Using the signal Aunt Jean had suggested to Grandma in case of an emergency, I banged on the bathroom pipe. When I heard my aunt speaking to her mother, I opened the door and stepped out of the bathroom. I sobbed, "She tried to stab me."

Grandma laughed, "She's lying again, Jean."

The front door opened and my mother came in. She saw I was crying and trembling.

"What's going on here?" she asked.

"Nothing," Grandma lied. And Jean described the situation to my mother.

I understood neither women wanted to believe their mother was crazy. I also realized one day this old woman might succeed in hurting me, or I would have to hurt her. Bewildered and unhappy, I closed my eyes and prayed to God for help. It calmed me.

When I opened my eyes I saw the dishtowel was extended beyond the chair's arm. *The knife must still fastened there under the strings.*

Calmly, I said, "If you don't believe your mother tried to stab me look under the dishtowel on the arm of her chair, and you'll see who's telling the truth."

Grandma screamed, "No!" and hunched her fat body over the towel. The two women hurried to the chair and struggled with her to pull away the towel.

They gasped on seeing a knife was holstered there.

"Ma! How could you do this? Why did you do this?" they asked, horrified.

I was relieved. *Now they knew I'm not the crazy one.*

"I'm not giving your mother insulin shots anymore. That's now your job. Keep her away from me."

Although I was late, I went to school. I didn't want to stay here with them. They needed time to figure out what to do next.

My teacher asked me for my late excuse. I didn't want, nor did I seek, sympathy. My prayer had been answered. *It's over now. What possible good can come from me telling her what had happened?* So, I lied. "My alarm clock didn't go off, and I overslept."

CHAPTER 23

A psychiatrist from Kings County Hospital, a state psychiatric institution, was in our apartment when I returned from school. I was told that he'd placed Grandma on a waiting list for admission to the hospital.

The doctor had suggested in the meantime she be kept in her room without her wheelchair. I was relieved to hear one day soon she wouldn't be living in the apartment.

**

Several weeks later, I came home to find my grandmother seated in the kitchen, on her wheelchair, talking with Aunt Jean.

"I took pity on my mother," Jean said, whining. "The doctor told me she has a moving blood clot. When it reaches her brain she could have psychotic episodes, or it could be fatal. Otherwise, she's normal."

"If that's the case, I refuse to come into the apartment unless she agrees to wheel to the far end of the kitchen giving me a clear path to the living room doorway."

In the months that followed, it felt like we played a mad version of pony express, or cowboys and Indians. As I would pass by the refrigerator, I'd grab a carton of milk and a loaf of bread and escape into the bedroom.

Grandma seemed to enjoy it, but I didn't. Mother didn't like me to sit on her living room furniture. It was for her company. So, I'd go directly into the rear bedroom we shared. I felt like a prisoner.

In the evening, Aunt Jean would bring her mother dinner. Uncle Joe would help get her into bed in the front bedroom. Afterwards, I would sit at the kitchen table to read, or do my homework.

On hearing Grandma start to chant, "God bless you," I'd close her bedroom door. It was difficult to study feeling frustrated and angry.

When my mother came home she'd bring three different kinds of left over pastries from the bakery where she worked. It was my dinner.

I gained weight, and my clothes became tight and tighter as I got fat and fatter. I was overweight yet I always felt hungry, and never satisfied.

One Saturday afternoon, mother took me to a store specializing in clothes for chubby girls. She selected a dress, skirt, and two sweaters.

"You better not gain more weight, Maxine. I can't afford to spend my money on clothes for you."

"Yetta, if you gave me money, I'd shop and prepare our meals." I wasn't aware Uncle Joe was giving her money to supplement her income.

She said, "Stop complaining. That's all you ever do around here."

In a way I envied Grandma, and wished I would be the one who'd soon live in another place.

CHAPTER 24

One day my economics teacher said, "If you should happen to buy a stock, be sure to check its progress with your broker, or in the newspaper."

The next day I phoned my broker. "How am I doing?"

"Fantastic. What a stock. You've already doubled your money."

"Well, that's good news."

I thought God had guided my choice. *He wants me to go to college.*

"I have another stock that might interest you, Miss Richard."

"No thank you. I have no money to invest right now."

All I had in my savings account was five dollars. I used my babysitting money to buy food at the marketplace around the corner. I did this so that I didn't have to eat the left-over stale cake my mother was constantly bringing home.

***

When I was hungry and had no money, I'd gather empty bottles from the vacant lot next door and return them to the grocer for their deposit. I munched on candy bars I bought or stole. I got fatter. After mother left for work, I borrowed her clothes from the closet to go to school when mine were too tight.

***

My mother had said I was smart enough to go to college. I knew I'd need to earn the money to do it. She lived hand-to-mouth, and had no money to pay for my tuition. I was counting on my stock to get me a college degree.

I saw *all my teachers were dressed well. A teacher must make good money. I'll become a teacher.* I hoped to earn a lot more money than my mother. I wanted to wear nice clothes, and eat real meals.

***

I was fifteen when the state mental hospital contacted Yetta to inform her there was a bed for her mother. The day Grandma was to leave, a psychiatrist and two men came to the apartment.

I was overjoyed when I saw them carrying her out the door, and shouted, "I'm glad you're going. I hope you never come back."

My mother attempted to hush me, but the doctor said, "Don't stop her. She's suffered a great deal. It's good for her to express what she feels."

Before the doctor left the apartment he handed me his card saying, "In case you feel like you need me, feel free to call."

I smiled and said, "With her gone, I'm going to be all right."

He said, "You're a courageous girl, Maxine."

CHAPTER 25

My economics teacher tried to explain arbitrage to the class. I was baffled by what he said. It made no sense to me.

I phoned my broker and told him what I thought it was, and then related the explanation I'd heard from my teacher. "Which is right?"

He took five minutes to carefully explain to me why I was correct, and told me that other person didn't understand arbitrage. "It's no wonder you picked ALCOA with your grasp of economics."

I felt flattered, but had no intention of correcting my teacher.

***

Yetta asked me to return a magazine to her sister. I brought it to Aunt Jeanr and she said, "You'll be sixteen next month. Are you going to get your working papers and go to work?"

"No. I'm going to college."

"Ha!" Uncle Joe laughed. "Maxine thinks she's smart, but she's really a dumb kid."

Hearing his opinion of me was hurtful. I didn't say anything to him. *My broker had told me I'm smart. However, I worried I might be over rating myself.*

I phoned my broker and mentioned my birthday was next month. He suggested taking me to dinner to celebrate. "By the way, how old will you be?"

"Sixteen."

"Sixteen! I had no idea you're only a kid. Who told you, you could get into the stock market?"

"My teacher told me. He said to buy a full coverage newspaper, pick a stock, and mail my money to my broker to pay for it."

"Well, there's a lot more to it than that… Listen, Maxine, now that I know you're a minor I have to put a legal guardian on your account, or sell you out."

"I need that money to go to college. Sell me out."

"Okay, I'll do it for you. Listen. Call me back when you're of legal age. You have the smarts required to be in the stock market. I haven't said that to many of my other customers. Goodbye, and good luck."

The following week, my mother showed me a letter that had arrived from my broker. It was addressed to me yet she'd opened it. She asked, "How come this company sent you this big check?"

"I put all my savings into the stock market."

"What's that?"

"A place where you can buy a share of a going business with your money. That check is for my college education."

Astounded, she handed me the check. I hurried to deposit the $1,500 into my savings account before she could think up a reason why she should have a share of it.

Meanwhile, she bragged to her sister about the money I'd earned. When I returned from the bank, Uncle Joe came upstairs and asked that I give him my money to help him buy this house for all of us to live in.

Live in a house with these people? No way. I planned to get a job and never see any of them again after I graduated from college. "Uncle Joe, I'm using my money to go to college."

"You were always a selfish girl, Maxine. Shame on you. You don't need to go to college. Don't you see that we could save rent money if we owned this house?"

"My mother works for menial pay because she didn't graduate from high school. She thinks I'm smart enough to go to college. I need to go to college to earn a good salary."

Joe left, slamming the door behind him.

In addition to babysitting, I got a job after school at the Five and Dime store. One day, Aunt Jean came in and selected several items. She walked over to my counter, and said, "Maxine, don't charge me for all of these things."

I realized that she was asking me for my cooperation to steal from my employer. I said, "I'm sorry, ma'am, but you'll need to go to another counter to pay for this merchandise."

***

Before I graduated from Samuel J. Tilden High School, the Guidance Counselor summoned me to her office.

"Your grade average isn't good enough for college. However, I see that you're capable of achieving A's. I'm going to approve your taking the Brooklyn College Scholarship exam if you insist."

"Thank you, Ma'am. I do want to take the exam." *God is my Counselor and more qualified than her.* "I'll let the college decide if I'm qualified to be a student there."

I knew it would be embarrassing if I didn't pass that exam. Bad enough if I should fail and not go to college, but to give Uncle Joe the opportunity to mock my effort would be humiliating. So, I didn't tell anyone I was going to take it.

It was three days of grueling tests on subjects I knew, and others that I didn't, until the exam was completed. I was surprised yet pleased when many students didn't return to take all the parts of the exam.

I thought it better to do my best, and not be a quitter. My back ached from the uncomfortable metal desk chairs we sat on while taking the exam. After that, we were told letters would be sent notifying those who were accepted, or not.

Later, I enjoyed walking around the well-groomed campus and beautiful gardens. There were trees, flowers, and bushes that I'd never before seen. A placard stated that the campus buildings were constructed in the same style as the prestigious College of William and Mary in Virginia.

Stopping by the business office, I was dismayed to learn the actual cost of a semester. Even if I were to pass the exam, the cost of credits and books would be more than I had in my bank account.

***

The following day, I woke with a swollen jaw and a raging toothache. My mother took me to a dentist. He said I had two impacted wisdom teeth and some deep cavities. *I felt I was being punished for stealing candy bars.*

He extracted the wisdom teeth, and scheduled me for other appointments. I was relieved that my mother hadn't opted to let the dentist pull out all my infected teeth to save her further dental bills.

In less than a week, the swelling had disappeared, and two cavities were filled.

When I came home from my job, Yetta met me at the door with a hug and a big smile on her face. "I have wonderful news. Brooklyn College has awarded you a partial scholarship."

I sighed, "Yetta, that's good news, and bad news."

"What do you mean?"

"I haven't got enough money to go to Brooklyn College even with the scholarship."

She said, wistfully, "No one in my family has ever gone to college."

"Yetta, you don't understand. The college accepted me. But I won't be able to go. I don't have enough money. And, without a degree, I'll never become a teacher."

"If I give you the money to go to college to become a teacher will you agree to give me half your salary?"

Hmm. Without her offer of help I foresaw a bleak future for me. *She's worked long hours and has supported me for years. I guess I owe her something. It was my fault that she divorced my father after I squealed on him. And, Dad is a cheat and a liar. I know I can't ever rely on him.*

So, I decided it would be fair to agree to share my salary with my mother. "Okay, Yetta, I promise to give you half my salary until I can repay you."

CHAPTER 26

College wasn't as hard as I thought it would be. I studied, did my class work, and made the Dean's List my freshman year.

One afternoon during that first year, Mrs. Hutt, one of the ladies for whom I had often babysat phoned. "My family has moved from Syracuse to Crown Heights. Please, Maxine, will you show my younger brother around the neighborhood?"

I said, "Okay," and I agreed to meet them at the luncheonette around the corner.

Mrs. Hutt was seated at a table with her son, Joel, and a handsome young man who had acne skin. She introduced us. "This is my brother, Martin Goldberg. You're the only person I know about his age."

Joel, who I knew was fond of me, came to stand beside me. I tousled Joel's hair, and smiled as I said, "Hi Martin, have you been to the library on Eastern Parkway?"

"We live across the street," he said. "My mother is in charge of the Famous Cafeteria on Eastern Parkway, on the corner of Utica Avenue.

I work there at night. Would you like to come over tonight to have dinner?"

Mrs. Hutt took Joel's arm. "Come to the counter, Son, and I'll buy you an ice-cream cone. Bye, Maxine. So long, Marty."

As they walked away, I said, "Thanks for the invitation Martin, but I'm on a diet."

"You eat food don't you?"

"Yes, of course."

"So come on over. It'll be my treat."

"I have to study for a test tomorrow."

"That's great. Bring your books. I'm the cashier at night, and bus when it's slow. You'll have plenty of time to study, and we'll be able to talk. Where do you go to school?"

"Brooklyn College."

"I went to Syracuse University before we moved down here. Now, I have to transfer to a college close by. I'd like to be a history professor when I graduate.

Until then, I help out my Mom by working nights at the cafeteria.

If you come at seven tonight that'd be perfect."

I couldn't resist his engaging smile, and the friendly expression in his warm brown eyes. "Okay. I'll be there, Martin."

***

The only thing wrong about Martin was his acne. I rarely had a pimple, and was worried what I would do if he tried to kiss me.

When my mother came home, I told her I'd been invited to dinner at the Famous Cafeteria.

"Oh, you got a rich boyfriend?"

"Not exactly. Martin is Mrs. Hutt's brother. I met him this afternoon. His mother is in charge of the cafeteria, and he's the night cashier."

"I'm going with you, Maxine. I'll have my dinner there, too. I don't want you to be walking alone at night."

Wow. Yetta cares about my safety. She must still love me. "Shall I introduce you as my sister?"

"Of course not. You'll introduce me to him as your mother."

She wants me to be her daughter again. I was ecstatic that she'd forgiven me for causing her divorce. I knew it had been difficult for her all these years. I smiled. "Okay, Mama."

CHAPTER 27

Mama and I walked arm in arm several blocks to the Crown Heights section where the cafeteria was located. Martin grinned and waved when he saw us coming toward him.

"Martin, this is my mother. She didn't want me to walk home alone in the dark."

"Pleased to meet you, Mrs. Richard. I planned to walk Maxine home after we close up here."

"Oh, I see. I didn't know that. You don't mind if I have dinner here too?"

Martin blushed with embarrassment before saying, "It's on the house."

I selected a table with good light to read by at the rear of the store. Mama said,

"I'll look after your books. You get what you want. I'll go after you come back." *Mama really cares about me.*

I placed a bowl of vegetable soup and a salad on my tray and went to the cashier. Martin asked, "Don't you want a slice of bread or a glass of milk?" I shook my head, and he let me pass on through to my table.

Mother took a tray to make her selections. I opened my book and began cramming for tomorrow's test.

Mama returned to the table with a tray laden with two orders of fish and three desserts. My jaw dropped. I was embarrassed that she'd helped herself to such an expensive meal on the house.

She gobbled up her food noisily then burped very loudly. Patrons turned around to stare at her. I felt mortified to have admitted to Martin that she was my mother.

Well satisfied, Mama patted her stomach and said, "Martin is walking you home. "There's no need for me to stay here."

She left, and didn't even stop to thank Martin for her meal, or say good night to him. *Martin won't want to see me again after tonight.* I was ashamed to be Mama's daughter. All these years I'd wanted her to proclaim that I was her daughter, and now I wanted to disclaim her as my mother.

It was hard enough to be the daughter of divorced parents and, thereby, considered to be a less desirable candidate to prospective in-laws. It didn't feel right that I was ashamed of my mother. A child is supposed to love her mother yet I didn't. I considered myself a selfish ingrate.

CHAPTER 28

M r. McNulty, my English professor, said one day, "Life is never boring. A bored person is mentally lazy and dull. In life you can re-write your own script. If you're unhappy with the one you're currently living with do something about it and change it!"

Hmm. I didn't like my current life script. Was it possible that I could change it?

A classmate, Lotus Chung, invited me to have lunch with her in the Sundial Garden that was beside the college library.

As we ate our sandwiches she said, "In China, a wise man selects a wife half his age plus ten years. What do you think of that?"

"Is that like an arranged marriage?"

"It could be considered so."

"I always thought that when you meet someone you really like, you get married."

"That may be the reason there're so many divorces in your country," she said.

"Adults should plan for their future together when they can afford to marry."
Hmm. Why did my parents get married? I think I'll ask my mother.

***

"Mama were you ever in love?"

"Yeah. I was sixteen. We went together for two years and then he suddenly up and married my best friend. I was shocked and hurt. All that time I thought that he loved me.

"Your grandmother explained it all to me. She said, 'Your friend's father owns a hardware store. Now, your old boyfriend has a steady job.'

"After they were married for a few months he came sniffing around my door again. I told the bastard to beat it!"

"Is that when you met my father and fell in love with him?"

"My mother hired your dad to install another bathroom in the house. Two families were living with her already. Mama boasted to him that she had lot's money.

Your father took me out a few times. He was a very good kisser. I decided to show the guy who jilted me that marriage was no big deal. I could easily get married too. So, when your dad proposed to me, I accepted.

"After we got married, my mother refused to pay him. However, she did let us move into the upstairs bedroom of her house."

Good grief. Without love it's no wonder that my parents got a divorce. I'm going to look around and try to figure out why people who've been married a long time have stayed together. I don't want to marry, and then get a divorce.

***

In the college curriculum I saw there was a course on marriage. I decided to take it in my junior year. I hoped that it would prepare me to have a lasting, happy marriage.

A few of the junior girls became engaged and dropped out of college. I overheard them brag, "I'm getting an MRS. That's what I came to college to get. I don't need to graduate."

Their fathers were businessmen and their parents weren't divorced. It occurred to me that I was yearning for the approval of a boyfriend's parents. I was longing to be a welcome part of a big happy family.

Then it occurred to me that I might get their approval, but would Mama pass muster? Involuntarily, I shuddered recalling the meeting of Martin Goldberg's mother and mine. Mrs. Goldberg had invited mother and me to join them at the Seder table in her newly decorated home. I'd never attended a traditional Seder. I found it very interesting, yet was embarrassed as my mother loudly stifled several yawns.

Tasty food was served, and Mama loaded up her plate as the dishes were passed around the table; taking seconds. She didn't comment on the delicious food yet gobbled it up like it was her last meal.

Then, at the end of the dinner, I was horrified to see her barf up her food spewing it over the table, rug upholstered chair, and me, seated beside her. I apologized to Mrs. Goldberg, and took my mother to the bathroom. I was mortified. I didn't return to the table after I'd cleaned us up.

***

Martin was unable to convince his mother that I was more like my father's side of the family. Soon after, we stopped seeing one another at his mother's insistence. I was depressed because the man I loved would never be mine.

I ate too much and wouldn't leave the house for several weeks except to go to school. Eventually, I started to date other young men, but I feared risking future incidents with my Mama.

Mama said, "Finish college and become a teacher. None of these boys you've been dating are worthy of you."

Mama and the marriage course started me to think it would be be wiser to marry a mature man who could support a family comfortably. I stopped dating college boys living at home. Therefore, it was no longer necessary for me to strive for the approval of my future in-laws, and they could meet Mama at the wedding.

I ran out of single businessmen to date in the neighborhood. None had met with Mama's high standards.

CHAPTER 29

Before graduation I learned most of my classmates were planning to take a prep course for the New York City Teacher's License Exam. It cost three hundred dollars. I didn't have the money. To get it, I took a job working Thursday night and all day Saturday at Macy's Department Store. I added these earnings to my meager savings account.

As a Macy employee I was given a discount card for any purchases I made at the store. We were told no one else was allowed to use this card.

One day Mama came to my counter. "Maxine, I need to buy a new dress. Give me your discount card."

"Mama, I'm not allowed to let anyone else use my card."

"What nonsense. I'm your mother. Give me the card," she insisted.

If Mama was caught using my card I'd be fired. I figured she'd feel guilty about getting me fired and give me the money I needed for the prep course.

So, I took the card from my purse under the counter and handed it to her,

A few minutes later she returned, accompanied by a Macy security employee, and I was fired on the spot. On the subway ride home, I told mother she should give me the money I needed to take the prep course since she'd gotten me fired from my job.

"What nonsense. You're smart enough to take the license exam without any prep course."

I was shocked by her cavalier attitude, and said, "Taking the exam may require more than me knowing my subject well."

"I'm not giving you any more money. Our deal was I give you the money to go to college period."

"Well, I hope I can pass the exam without taking the prep course." "Oh, you will. I have faith in you, Maxine."

Thanks, Mama.

***

I tried to get tips from my classmates who took the course, but no one would discuss anything about it with me. If I'd shelled out three hundred dollars then I'd be tight-lipped too.

The day of the exam, paper was passed out to the candidates. We were told to raise our hands if we needed more paper. I carefully answered each question, filling every line of the three yellow sheets.

During the test, it surprised me to see how many people raised their hands to get more yellow papers. I noticed one person had scrawled only five lines on each sheet of paper. I was puzzled.

The test was fair, and I knew most of the answers. I thought I might've passed the exam without benefit of the prep course.

After the license exam was over I overheard someone boast, "I took care to write very large on each sheet of paper since the examiners allow only three grammar errors on each page."

Uh-oh. By writing on each line of the sheets, I had probably exceeded the three mistakes per page limit.

CHAPTER 30

"**G**randma misses you," Mama said. "She wants to see you, Maxine. Please come with me to the hospital this Sunday."

"No. I don't miss her."

"She's an old woman. You'll never forgive yourself if she dies without her seeing you."

"No thanks. I'll risk it."

"Don't be flip with me young lady. She's my mother and I love her. It's no wonder that she's in a mental facility. She had a very difficult life."

"Really? I know she gave me a difficult time."

"Be nice for a change, Maxine. Do something nice for someone else. You don't want to think you're a terrible person. Don't be so selfish. Aren't you ashamed for what you said when they came and took your Grandma away? This may be your last chance to apologize to her."

"Apologize for what? Telling the truth?" *That old woman never thought about anyone but herself. When I was a youngster she left me alone every day in the locked apartment. She kept the money you gave her to pay that man Schultz. Then, she left me as his "pay" for the man she well-knew was a pedophile.*

I wondered what this woman had done to elicit such caring from her daughters?

As far as I knew, Grandma was a nut job, and that's why she was where she was. It was a great relief to me she no longer lived in our apartment. *Hmm. If I agree to go, I'll get my deluded mother off my back. Who knows? Perhaps, with medication and treatment, my sick Grandma is a person worthy of such devotion.*

That woman I have yet to meet.

"Okay Mama, I'll go along with you this Sunday."

"Oh, I'm so glad. You'll feel better about yourself now, Maxine. I'm sure of it. I'll take you to lunch before we see her. Won't that be nice?

***

Spending a pleasant time with Mama was worth the effort. We entered the reception room of the hospital. I saw Grandma no longer looked sallow and scary. She had lost more than fifty pounds. I was glad for her. I walked over to give her a perfunctory kiss. She grabbed hold of me.

"You think you're smart because you're going to be a teacher. Well, my children take care of me. You read books, but you don't know how to cook or sew. No man is ever going to want you for a wife." She grinned, "You're going to be an old maid schoolteacher. I'm smarter than you. No one will be there to take care of you when you're old. You'll live with your Mama forever," she said, and cackled.

***

I wouldn't give her the satisfaction of seeing that her words wounded me. I smiled and said, "Thanks for your good wishes, Grandma." Her smile vanished.

She hadn't changed. What a hateful old bitch to say those mean things to me. I was sorry I'd come, and would never come here again.

I looked over at my smiling mother and suspected she'd brought me here to be verbally beat up by my Grandma. I wished I could throw up my lunch all over her to retaliate.

After that experience, I promised myself I would never use my children to my advantage when I married. A month later Grandma died, and I went to her funeral. I sat Shiva with the rest of her family, but I didn't miss her, or shed a tear.

***

The letter I'd been awaiting from the Board of Education came. I stared at the envelope and dreaded opening it. Mama grabbed it from my hands and ripped it open.

"You failed," she shrieked. "You're an educated bum just like your father"

I went to bed and cried. I knew if I'd taken the prep course I'd have passed the exam easily. What would I do now? I prayed for guidance and fell asleep

***

The hoot of a passing train awakened me. The thought occurred to me that trains, not just subways traveled in and out of the city each day. *That's it! I'll look for a teaching job on Long Island.*

***

I took the subway to Penn Station where the commuter trains arrived in New York City, and purchased a copy of the Long Island Press. Turning to the want ads I saw there was a position open for an elementary school teacher in Lindenhurst, Long Island. I had no idea where that was. I phoned the number to ask if I might interview for the job.

The position was still open. A round-trip-ticket cost me all the money I had in my purse. The clerk told me Lindenhurst was forty-five minutes away in Suffolk County. I wanted to get that teaching job, and nothing else mattered.

***

Aboard the train, I searched my pockets and purse for coins. I hadn't eaten any breakfast before I left home and was hungry. I watched as we passed through various towns; each succeeding one looking less and less crowded. At last the train pulled into Lindenhurst.

CHAPTER 31

I learned the Office of the Superintendent of Schools was fifteen blocks from the train station. I decided to take a bus to my appointment, and make the return trip on foot to conserve my pennies. I had fifteen cents left in my purse to buy food.

After a brief interview, the superintendent offered me a contract to teach third grade. I happily signed it. *I have a job. I'm not an educated bum like my father.*

I walked back to the station and bought two apples and a banana at the grocery store next to the station. As I sat munching my second apple, reality sank in. Yes, I had a teaching job. But, it required two hours of travel each way plus train fare for me to live at home in Brooklyn.

I'll have to move to this small town and live here. Oh, my goodness. This wasn't what I'd planned on when I agreed to give Mama half my salary. *I'll need to pay rent, and buy food with only half of my teaching salary. I could wind up living on less than what my mother now earns.*

***

"Mama, I have good news, and bad news.

"What's the good news?"

"I'm the third-grade teacher of the School Street School on School Street in Lindenhurst, Long Island. I start on Monday."

"Well, that is good news. So, what's the bad news?"

"When I agreed to pay you half my salary I thought I'd be living here with you. However, this job requires me to live in Lindenhurst…

"Just a minute young lady" she interrupted, "It's not my fault you aren't smart enough to pass the license exam and teach in New York City. A deal is a deal."

It was obvious that she didn't care I'd have expenses I hadn't foreseen. "Okay, I'll give you half my salary until I've repaid what I owe."

"No. That's not enough. A deal is a deal."

"Sorry, but that wasn't part of the deal we agreed to Mama."

"I'm your mother! Don't you feel you owe me for all I've done for you?"

"Not really."

"Is that so. Well, I threw your father out once. Now, you can get out of my house, too. Go find somewhere else to stay."

Mama was renting out the front bedroom. I couldn't share her bed. So, I walked across the street to Katy Fisherkelli's house; a friend of mine.

Katy was delighted to see me and hugged and kissed me. Mrs. Fisherkelli insisted that I stay for dinner. She filled my plate with spaghetti and meatballs. She told me how grateful she was I had tutored Katy for free. No one was surprised I'd gone on to college, and was now was a teacher.

I didn't want to burden them with my woes. I lied, "I left my house key in Lindenhurst and have no place to sleep tonight."

"Stop. Don't say another word… You'll sleep in the twin bed in Katy's room. My daughter, Theresa, got married last month and moved out. There's a spare bed here for you any time you want it."

"Thank you, so much. I really do appreciate your offer and I'm happy to accept… if it's all right with you Kate?"

"Sure…I miss talking to someone before I go to sleep."

***

Kate heard me sobbing and turned on the bedroom lamp. She came to my bed. "What's wrong? Why are you crying?"

I looked up, and, through my tears, saw a halo of light around her lovely face. *She's an angel.* I explained all that had happened since we'd graduated from high school; including the deal I'd made with my mother.

Kate gave me tissues and said, "You've got some mother. My house is your house. Come and stay here as often as you like."

Mrs. Fisherkelli prepared a delicious breakfast of bacon and eggs. I went to the bank and withdrew fifty dollars from my savings account before returning to my mother's apartment to pack my clothes. The train took me to

Lindenhurst, and I searched the local newspaper to find a place to live.

A room was for rent in the home of a Mrs. Sporel was available. I phoned and explained to her I was a new elementary school teacher in town, and I needed a place to live. She offered to pick me up at the station.

At her house, she showed me a large bedroom with a study. Her son had gone off to college, she said. She was lonely, liked company, and wanted to make a few dollars. We agreed on fifteen dollars for the monthly rent, and I could use half of a shelf in her refrigerator.

She made tea and chatted on and on about the feats of her athletic son. She filled my lonely hours all week with her talking. I didn't mind.

However, on Sunday, she expected me to go to church with her. I told her I was a Jewess, and I didn't attend church.

"Oh, did you have your horns removed?" she asked.

"What?" I asked in surprise. "I've never had horns. Jews don't have horns."
"Oh yes they do."

She got her Bible from a shelf to prove to me Jews have horns. I looked at the drawing she showed me. It did depict a man with horns. The text stated he was a Jew. *I liked my room. I had be diplomatic yet honest with her if I planned to stay.*

"Mrs. Sporel, I can see why you thought Jews have horns. However, I've never seen a Jew with horns. I've never ever heard of Jews having horns 'til now."

She squinted her eyes and asked, "Were both your parents Jews?"

"Yes."

"I have to go now, or I'll be late for church."

She marched out of the room. I'd never encountered a person who thought Jews had horns. I'd grown up in a neighborhood with Italians and Jews. I wasn't accustomed to feeling any different from anyone else because I was Jewish.

The thought occurred to me there might not be any other Jews in this small town. *Who will I date around here?*

I recalled Grandma's dreadful prediction that I'd die an old maid schoolteacher with no one to care for me. *It was a fearful possibility if I remained here.* In Lindenhurst, I was out of the "rat race."

Oh dear God, until I repay my mother I'm stuck here. How will I ever find a man to love and marry? Please help me.

***

There was a letter in my school mailbox. It was from my mother. Scrawled across the sheet of paper was written, "Where's my money?"

I wrote Mama that teachers in Lindenhurst are paid every two weeks. When I got my money, she would get a check. I was eager to start paying down what I owed her. I mailed the letter on my way home.

At Mrs. Sporel's house, I found she'd rented the study to Kim, another new teacher for ten dollars. I didn't argue with Mrs. Sporel she'd already rented it to me. *Let her be the money grubbing one that Jews are supposed to be.*

Kim had a car and taught at a school a short distance from mine. *"I'll help you pay for her gas, and get a lift going to and coming back from work."* She agreed.

Kim was an amiable girl. It didn't matter to me that Mrs. Sporel told me she wasn't a Jew. However, Kim confessed to me that she was Jewish, but didn't want it known in town.

"When in Rome do as the Romans" she said.

So, Kim went to church with Mrs. Sporel. She met men and dated frequently, while I sat at home alone, feeling lonely.

***

I completed my lesson plans three months ahead of time. I could bear my loneliness no longer. I bought a round-trip ticket, and went back to Brooklyn.

***

When I arrived at the apartment, I was surprised to find my Uncle Al was now occupying the front bedroom with his "war bride." Her name was Sigrum.

He told me my mother was very happy with the checks I was sending her.

"At the moment she's in Atlantic City "visiting a friend.""

Humph. Someone's having a good time with the money I'm earning.

There was no opportunity for me to see Mama during this trip. I consoled myself by eating half of the chocolate cake in the refrigerator.

***

I left Mama a note stating I wanted to see her to renegotiate our agreement. A few days later I found a letter in my school mailbox. "No!" it said, and nothing more.

Another month passed, I was so lonely I considered going to church with Kim to meet and date young men.

Then, I read in the Long Island Press there were synagogues on the Island that held socials. However, I couldn't convince Kim to go to one of their dances. I considered the train fare plus the price of admission too expensive for me to attend.

So, I decided to go home and try once more to reason with my unreasonable mother for a reduction in the money I was giving her.

This time Mama was home. I was shocked to see how much weight she had gained. "How come you've let yourself go?"

"I'm not fat. I'm pregnant."

"I hope you're getting married soon."

"No. The father of the child is a married man. I'm going to have it, and tell everyone it's your baby."

"What?" I asked and was flabbergasted by her news. "I'm not going to have anything further to do with you after I repay you."

"You're an only child, Maxine. Are you so selfish that you don't want to have a sister or brother?"

I didn't bother to respond to that ridiculous question, but said, instead, "Are you so dense you don't understand you no longer have a daughter?"

Disgusted with her, and too angry for any more words I left. I went to see my friend Kate.

CHAPTER 32

Kate was getting ready to go ice skating at the Iceland Rink at Madison Square Garden. "Come with me, Maxine. You look to me like you need to exercise more."

Kate was correct. I'd regained five of the fifteen pounds I'd lost consoling my loneliness with chocolates.

We took the subway. As I stood holding onto the pole of the rocking car. I prayed for guidance and a solution to my dilemma.

When we arrived at Penn Station, I told Kate that I would take the last train back to Lindenhurst, and not sleep at her house.

Kate was a very good figure skater. She owned her skates. I could barely stand on my rented ones. She helped me lace my boots with her hook, and supported me as we circled the ice rink. I told Kate how worried I was about meeting a nice man living in the suburbs.

I thought she was listening without commenting. However, when a very handsome young man skated up to us. "Hi Katy," he said. "Want to skate with me?"

Kate smiled and nodded. Then, she steered me to a bench outside the rink. "Maxine, you sit there. Tony works in the office next to mine. I've been dying to meet him. This is my first real chance to get to know him."

"Ask him if he's got a friend," I called out as she skated away.

I worked hard at tightening my loosened skate laces. It was difficult on my fingers, and they were aching.

A shadow fell across my white boot. I looked up and saw a handsome, clean-scrubbed skinny man at the rink rail. He asked, "Will you skate with me?"

I was certain, from his appearance and this charitable act of asking an overweight girl to skate he was a priest on a retreat who'd taken pity on me. I smiled at the slender man and said, "Thank you for asking, but I don't think that you can support me."

He laughed. "I'd like to try. I'm a lot stronger than I look." Then, he extended his hand to me and he managed to get me onto the ice and hold me close. I was surprised to feel bulging arm muscles beneath his cable sweater. I felt safe and secure with him. We passed Kate and Tony. She looked surprised to see me skating with my shining white knight.

We glided effortlessly around the rink. He told me his name was Irving Feller, and I was glad to learn he wasn't a priest.

Irving introduced me to the friends who had convinced him to come here tonight. Then, Kate, without Tony, skated over to us. I introduced her to Irving, and his friends. She left us to skate with one of them. Then, Irving asked me to have coffee with him after the skating session.

I told him I needed to catch the last train to Lindenhurst at 9:45. He suggested we leave the rink as soon as I said "goodbye" to Kate.

CHAPTER 33

I felt pleased to have met this man. However his olive complexion led me to believe he was Italian, and I wanted to date a Jewish man.

We talked for quite a while at a nearby coffee shop. And I enjoyed our conversation. When he asked to see me the following week I said, "I like you a lot Irving, but you're not Jewish. I don't want to start something I feel has no future for me."

"Maxine, you're Jewish? I thought you were Irish. I'm Jewish too." We laughed together. "Look here, it's not necessary for you to take the train to Lindenhurst. I have a car, and I'll be glad to drive you home."

"It's a very long way. I don't want you to be late for work tomorrow."

"I'm a businessman. My brothers and I own a store. No one will object if I come in late."

"What kind of store do you have?"

"Feller's Department Store. It's on 125th Street and Amsterdam Avenue in Harlem. I'm parked two blocks from here. Let's go now."

Walking alongside Irving, I could hardly believe my good fortune to have met this Jewish "mench." I recalled my prayer on the subway. *Thank You, Lord for answering it.*

We arrived at his black DeSoto. He opened and held the door for me. I said,

"I bet you like Groucho Marx."

He laughed and said, "Yes. He's my favorite comedian."

"Mine too."

Seated behind the wheel he asked, "How do I get to Lindenhurst?"

"I don't know how to drive there. I always take the train."

"That's all right. I'll stop at the gas station on East 92nd Street, and they'll give me the directions"

Wow. Irving knows how to take care of difficulties as they pop up. I liked that about him. I thought here's someone I can rely on.

While the tank was being filled at the station by the attendant, Irwin spoke to the man in the office to get the directions to Lindenhurst.

"Once there, I'd be able to direct you to where I live."

As he drove along the Sunrise Highway, I asked Irving to tell me about himself. He did. He talked for a solid hour. Afterward, he said, "You're an easy person for me to talk to. Please come out with me Saturday night?"

"Yes. I'd like to see you again, Irving."

"We'll have dinner and go dancing."

"That sounds very nice."

We arrived in Lindenhurst, and I directed him to the house where I lived. The lights were still on inside. He walked me to the door, but I didn't invite him in. He asked, "Will I have to drive out here to pick you up for our date next week?"

"No." And I wrote down Mama's Brooklyn address, and gave it to him with the telephone number.

"I'll see you Saturday night at eight o' clock for dinner and dancing."

The front door opened, and Mrs. Sporel stood there. "Hello. I thought I heard voices out here. Won't you come in?"

"This is my boyfriend, Irving Feller. Thank you for the invitation but he has a long trip back to New York City."

Irving grinned, and shook her hand. He kissed me goodnight on the cheek, and left.

"He seems very nice," she said. "But don't you think he's a little old for you?" "I think he's just perfect for me. Goodnight."

CHAPTER 34

After school Friday, I walked to the train station. The dress shop on Main Street was having a "Going Out of Business Sale". I'd admired the owner's selection of stylish dresses in the window many times, but was unable to afford one. I wanted to buy a date dress for Saturday night. I wondered if I might be able to afford one on sale and went in.

I asked the saleswoman for a black dinner dress in size fourteen. She brought out a red dress. "I'm sorry Miss, but this is the only dress I have left in your size."

I was disappointed. The dress was modest yet stylish and the fabric felt nice to the touch. Well, *I might as well try it on, but I don't care for the color.*

I went into the dressing room and dropped the silk taffeta dress over my head. I twirled. It had a daring low cut back. I loved it.

"I'm on a tight budget. How much is this dress?" I asked.

"I'm the owner. I know no one around here is going to buy it. I'll let you have it for ten dollars."

"Thank you. I'll take it."

I took the train to Penn Station. It occurred to me that my new dress deserved a matching lipstick, and bought one at the drug store. I wanted to look my best for Irving tomorrow night.

I unlocked the door of my mother's apartment. Uncle Al told me she'd gone to stay with friends for a few weeks. I was glad she wasn't there.

Al's wife was a pretty girl but a messy housekeeper. I hung my new dress in the rear bedroom closet, and changed my clothes.

Wearing dungarees and a sweater, I vacuumed the living room rug, polished the furniture, scrubbed the tiled bathroom and linoleum in the kitchen, and washed, dried, and put away all the dishes in the sink. After that, I bathed, washed my hair, and set it. I wanted everything to look nice for Irving.

***

Saturday afternoon, I was giving myself a manicure when Kate knocked on the door. "Thank goodness you're all right, Maxine."

"What do you mean?"

"Nick, one of those boys you introduced me to at the Iceland said Irving told them that he was going to marry you. No sane person says that when he meets someone brand new."

I laughed and said, "Irving's not crazy. He does the buying at his department store. So, he may know just what he wants when he sees it. He may be the smartest man I've ever met."

"Would you be willing to marry him?"

"I don't know that yet. I just met the man. I like him a lot. We have a date for tonight. If he acts weird then I won't see him again. Thanks for the information."

Hmm. I'd heard about love at first sight, but never thought it would happen to me. It was nice to know Irving's intentions were honorable. He hadn't yet met Mama. He might change his mind.

I knew she would find fault with him if she thought I was the least bit interested in marrying him. I was now onto her game, "No one's good enough for my college-educated daughter meal ticket." She wanted me to wind up an old maid… To heck with her plan for me.

CHAPTER 35

Irving arrived promptly at eight. He looked well-scrubbed and wore a blue suit. He presented me with a corsage. *Wow. How thoughtful to bring me flowers.* I invited him to sit in the living room while I walked to the bedroom to pin them on.

He complimented me on my dress. "Where are we going?" I asked.

"The Copacabana."

Wow. It was the nicest nightclub in Manhattan. I was glad I'd bought a new dress.

***

Irving found a parking place on Fifth Avenue, and we walked to the club. Then, we waited in the lounge enjoying the music playing by the band until our table was ready. Everyone looked relaxed amidst the glass fruits decorating the room. *I thought this would be a great place to have a Succoth party.*

***

We were led to our table by the waiter who gave us menus. I was thrilled to learn Tony Martin would be performing here tonight. He was my favorite singer. *Wow. Irving must be a very successful businessman to be able to afford this place.* I was in seventh heaven to know that he'd said he wanted to marry me.

Irving ordered steaks. We danced while waiting for them. I felt very comfortable in his strong arms, and said, "Your muscles are so large. Do you lift weights?"

He laughed. "No. Before I started to work at the store I carried sides of meat and delivered them to butcher shops around the city."

Our food came to the table before the show. We were eating it when a man wearing a tuxedo stopped at our table. He said, "Give Florence my regards."

Irving said, "I haven't seen her for several months."

The man smiled and nodded. Then, he went to a table on the other side of the dance floor.

I asked, "Who's Florence?"

"My wife."

The food stuck in my throat, and I couldn't swallow. I didn't want to be involved with a married man. I gulped. "What? You never told me that you were married." *I felt as if a rug had just been pulled out from under me.*

"I'm getting a divorce from her."

Oh, yeah…. I've read stories about men who tell girls they're getting a divorce. I'm not going to fall for that old line. I no longer trusted him. He wants to string me along and raise my hopes just like my father. He's a rat, too. I lost my appetite.

The house lights dimmed. My favorite singer, Tony Martin, entered the circle of blue light next to the piano and started to sing.

I was glad the room was dark. I didn't want Irving to see there were tears in my eyes. I considered my situation while Tony performed. *This is a nice place he's taken me. The food's very good. Tony Martin's great. No need to act like a fool and make a scene.*

I just won't go out with him again after tonight… I said nothing about what was on my mind as Irving drove me home.

"Thank you for a lovely evening, Irving. Goodbye."

"Goodbye? What's the matter? Aren't you going to kiss me goodnight?"

"No. I don't kiss married men."

"I'm getting a divorce from Florence."

"When will the decree be final?" *No man is going to string me along.*

"In two months," he said.

Hmm. He gave me a time limit. Could it be that he's telling me the truth? No. My father made promises, too. I can't trust the promises of men like him… I refuse to be like my mother and carry on an affair with a married man.

"Good. I'm happy to hear that. I like you, Irving. In two months you may call me if you're divorced."

Then, I hurried to the apartment, closed the door, and locked it. Irving had followed me and knocked on the door. I didn't open it. I asked, "What do you want?"

"Will it be all right if I telephone you before the two months are up? I really enjoy talking to you."

"Yes, that'll be all right. You may call me." *He sounds so sweet and sincere, or is he just a good actor? I hoped he was telling me the truth.*

CHAPTER 36

I forgot Irving only had my mother's telephone number in Brooklyn. I hadn't given him Mrs. Sporel's phone number in Lindenhurst. I didn't get any phone calls from him, and I was disappointed. So, I decided to chalk the incident up to experience.

Oh well, dreams don't always come true. I tried to forget about what might've been.

***

Kim, my roommate, confided to me she'd missed her period, and thought she might be pregnant. *I was surprised a sexually active girl hadn't used protection.*

"Do you want to marry your boyfriend? Have you told him about it?"

"My parents wouldn't like it if I married out of my faith."

"Would they prefer you be an unwed mother?"

"I guess not. I see Jim Saturday night. I'll tell him… and see what he says."
"That's a good idea."

***

Sunday morning, Kim went to church with Jim Smith. She told me he'd said, if I'd convert then he'd marry me. I was surprised she'd revealed to him that she was Jewish since she'd attended church regularly with him. I wondered if a marriage starting out with lies could succeed.

Kim moved out the following day to live with Jim. I wished her well.

Although I didn't practice my religion, I did want to marry a Jew. I hoped to learn more about observing Jewish traditions after I married. I wanted to be a good Jewish wife and mother.

***

Coughs and sniffles went up and down the rows of my classroom. I caught the worst cold I'd ever had. It wasn't until six weeks later, just before Thanksgiving, that I revisited Brooklyn.

93

Mama no longer appeared to be pregnant. I decided not to ask her about it. Whatever she did, I decided was none of my business. However, I was glad she no longer appeared to be with child. Having Yetta for a mother was something that I wouldn't wish on anyone else.

Mama asked, "Who's Irving Feller? He called here several times to speak to you."

"He's a guy I met when I went ice skating."

"He sounds nice. Are you interested in him?"

"He was a good date." Actually, I was very glad to hear he did call me. Then, I remembered I'd only given him my Brooklyn phone number.

However, I concealed my feelings behind a book. I'd had plenty of time to review what Grandma had said to me. Although she wanted to lord it over me that she was the clever one, and I the stupid one.

After I got over my initial anger at being laughed at, and played for a fool, then I realized she'd tipped me onto their game. Mama did want me to be an old maid school-teacher. That's why no one would ever be "good enough for her daughter".

"Oh, you went out with him already?"

"Yes. He took me to the Copacabana for dinner."

"Fancy place. He was a good date."

"Yes."

"If he calls again do you want me to tell him you don't want to go out with him again?"

I yawned and answered, "Oh, I'd go out with him again."

It was obvious Mama was trying to find out whether or not I was interested in this man. If I were to indicate any interest she'd be sure to say, or do something obnoxious when she met him to discourage him.

The phone rang, and she answered it. "It's him," she said, and handed me the receiver… Mama lingered in the room to overhear my conversation.

"Hi, Irving."

"Maxine, it's only two more weeks until my divorce decree becomes final.

Please go out with me. I think about you all the time. I really want to see you."

"All right, but I'll have to check my calendar first." I was intent on keeping our conversation short and casual for Mama's benefit. I was unaware I was at the same time peaking Irving's interest in me.

"May I take you to Number One Fifth Avenue for Thanksgiving Dinner?"

"Let me check… Yes. Irving that'll be fine. What time will you pick me up?"

"Is two o'clock okay?"

"Two is good. I'll see you then."

When I hung up the phone, Mama appeared satisfied he was no one special to me.

"When are you going to see him?"

"Two o'clock on Thanksgiving Day. He's taking me to dinner."

"Where?"

"A restaurant on Fifth Avenue. Mama, please excuse me, I have these tests to grade." That ended her questioning… for now.

***

On Thanksgiving Day, Mama opened the door to Irving when he knocked. He arrived a little early. He carried a bouquet of colorful seasonal leaves and chrysanthemums.

Mama gasped, "You look like Rudolph Valentino." I didn't know who that was., I assumed he was a silent movie star.

"Irving, this is my mother."

"How do you do, Mrs. Reichard."

I took the flowers to put them in a vase. "I'll get my sweater."

"Where are you taking my daughter?"

"Number One Fifth Avenue."

"Won't you come into the living room and sit awhile Irving?"

"Thank you, but we have a reservation for three o'clock."

"Well, you children can just run along. I'll open up a can of soup for my dinner."

"Mrs. Reichard, if you've no other plans why don't you come along with us?" "You're sure that's all right?"

"It will be my pleasure to escort two beautiful ladies to dinner."

I was impressed with Irving's diplomacy. I was surprised he *was able to handle my mother with such aplomb. It's no wonder he's such a successful businessman.*

Mama didn't attempt to get into the front seat with my date. *Well, she has some sense of decorum.*

At the restaurant, Mama seated herself between Irving and me. I noticed she touched his arm several times. "Irving, you may call me, Yetta." *Was she making a move to steal my date?*

When Mama went to the restroom, Irving got down on one knee and asked me to marry him. He'd pulled the rug out from under me once. I feared to be hurt again.

"Irving, I really don't know you well enough to say "yes", or "no". Please get up before Mama comes back." He did and said, "I can wait until you know me better. What would you like for an engagement gift?"

I was flabbergasted. I felt wary of Irving. He was very sure of himself. *He seemed to be a good catch for any woman, but so was Howard Hughes, and he's still single.*

Is Irving toying with me? How will I know if I love him enough to marry him? I never want to be divorced. I'll need more time to get to know him. Two dates is not enough time for me,

As we drove homeward, Mama commented on how beautiful the foliage in the Catskill Mountains must be at this time of year.

Irving surprised us when he said, "If you like, Yetta, I can drive you up to Fallsburg right now, and pick you up next week and return you home."

"Oh, that would be just wonderful, Irving. I'll pack a few things as soon as we get home," she said smiling slyly at him.

She bolted from the car as soon as Irving parked. She had no intention of letting the offer of a free round-trip ride to the Catskills Mountain area pass her by. While we waited for her to return, Irving and I talked in the car. "Why are you being so nice to my mother?"

"It can't hurt to be nice to my future mother in law. How's about a kiss for doing my good deed?"

Irving may very well be the smartest fellow I've ever met. He knows how to handle my mother better than I do. I gave him my Lindenhurst phone number.

Irving had put his cards on the table, and I wanted to be fair to him. Recalling what Grandma said, I warned him, "Irving, I don't cook, or sew, and I don't like to do housework."

"I don't like doing those things either. I'll get you a maid. There's another room in the house I'm far more interested in."

I grinned and felt certain Grandma must be turning over in her grave. I kissed him, and he kissed me. After that, I gave him Mrs. Sporel's telephone number.

Irving said, "The next few weeks I'll be busy buying, and selling at the store during the Christmas holidays. Please save New Year's Eve for me."

"I will."

"I'm hoping you'll give me your answer then."

"Irving, when I marry I want it to be for keeps. I don't ever want to be divorced."

"Well, I'm glad you feel that way about marriage. You take your time making up your mind. I want you to be sure."

Irving understands my position, and is respectful of my honesty and feelings. All I have to do now is understand my own feelings, and determine if I love him.

What is love anyway? If I'm feeling sick I can take my temperature to determine if I'm sick, and how bad it is. I know I like Irving a lot. I know he works hard and is successful. I like that he has brothers. I always wanted to part of a large loving family like the Fisherkellis.

CHAPTER 37

The phone rang and I answered it. I was shocked to hear the voice of Martin Goldberg, my old flame. *Mama must have given him my number here in Lindenhurst. Why?* "How are you, Martin?"

"It was a mistake for me not to continue seeing you, Maxine. I haven't met anyone I like as much as you. I was wondering what you're doing New Year's Eve?"

"I already have a date for New Year's Eve. I'm glad you still consider us friends. However, I've met someone I'm seriously considering marrying him. *You broke my heart once, Martin. You won't get another chance.*

"Oh? I didn't know that. Well, I wish you the best of luck, Maxine. Do I know the lucky guy?"

"I doubt it. He lives in Manhattan."

"Well, if you should decide not to marry him then please call me. I have a job now, and no longer live with my mother."

"I'm happy for you, goodbye." *It felt good to dismiss him from my life. Why did Mama give him this phone number? She certainly did her best to break us up last year.*

Returning to my mother's apartment, I saw she was no longer renting the front bedroom. It annoyed me my money was enabling her to enjoy a telephone, and her privacy. *I looked forward to the time when I'd be able to enjoy the fruits of my labor.*

Mama came out of the bedroom. "Hi, Maxine. I met your old boyfriend in the library. I gave him your number. He was such a nice young man. Why didn't you continue to see him?"

You have a convenient memory I thought. I said, "It didn't work out."

"He's a lot closer to your age than Irving. Are you aware that by marrying a man much older than you, you'll be sure to end up a young widow?"

"You're probably right, Mama. We're just friends." I tried my best to keep her off the scent of what I felt for Irving.

"I think Irving's a lot closer to my age than your age."

"I guess he is. Why don't you date him?"

"He hasn't asked me out yet. Would you mind if I did date him?"

"Why would I mind?" I was starting to enjoy playing this cat and mouse game. Mama had no idea what my feelings were. I knew she wished Irving were attracted to her. After that I realized she was jealous of me.

Was it Irving's good looks? No. It was probably the nice places he could afford to take me. I didn't tell Mama I already had a date with him on New Year's Eve.

Mama said, "Irving doesn't call here anymore."

"Christmas is coming. He's probably busy at the store." "I forgot about his store. Do you know the name of it?" "No." I said, and picked up a book to read.

"Why not?"

"If you want, I'll ask next time I see him. *I hope she doesn't get it into her head to go over there. I don't want her bothering him. Mama is too good at being obnoxious when it suits her.*

The fact that I was this concerned about Irving made me realize that I cared about him. Maybe, I was in love with him. I continued to read my book, and she left the room.

CHAPTER 38

On New Year's Eve, Irving took me to the Empire Room at the Waldorf Astoria. Trini Lopez was performing. As we sipped our champagne just before midnight, he asked, "Maxine, are you any closer to making a decision about us?"

If I say yes, will he spring another surprise on me? I don't want to get hurt again, and I don't want to lose him by saying no.

"Irving, I love you, and I'll marry you. But first, I have to repay my mother."

"What do you mean?"

"Mama lent me the money to go to college. Until I pay back what I owe her, I can't stop working. I agreed to give her half of my teaching salary.

"Is that the only obstacle that stands in the way of our getting married?"

"Yes."

"Whew! I thought you wanted her to live with us. Don't worry, Maxine. I'll straighten things out with your mother. Now, what would you like me to give you for an engagement gift? A ring?"

Might something else interfere with our wedding? If he were to give me a ring I'd be obliged to return it if we didn't get married. That would put me back to square one. I want something tangible to hold onto that would enable me to meet other eligible Jewish men in case he changes his mind.

"No, I don't want a ring. I'm concerned about your speeding tickets on the Triborough Bridge. A car makes better sense to me. Don't you agree?"

Irving grinned, "I'm seven years older than you, Maxine. I didn't know how to tell you how exhausted I feel after I drive back home from Lindenhurst. You must love me a lot to be so thoughtful and considerate. Most women would rather have a diamond to show off to their friends. I'll be happy to give you a car."

Patrons all around the nightclub started to toot their horns. It was midnight, and the band played Auld Lang Syne. Balloons fell from the ceiling. Irving took me in his arms and held me close, and we kissed.

Then the band played a Mexican-flavored version of "Bye, bye Blackbird," and we danced 'til closing time.

Irving asked, "Shall I rent a room for us at this hotel tonight?"

I recalled what I'd once read in Lao Tse's book, "The orange from the silver bowl on the table once used is soon tossed into the waste basket."

"Honey, we're not married yet. Please, drive me home."

CHAPTER 39

O n Monday, after school, I signed up for driving lessons. If I were going to get a car then I wanted to know how to drive it.

I had not phoned Mama to tell her I'd agreed to marry Irving. When I returned to Brooklyn, I was genuinely shocked to hear her say, "Maxine, if you don't invite your father, then I'll pay for your wedding."

I realized Irving must've spoken to her. *Did he convince her to forgive my debt?*

My father was as good as dead to me, but he wasn't dead. Irving's family would think it peculiar if my father weren't present at my wedding.

I didn't care whether or not he came. But I thought it incorrect not to invite him. *I'll talk it over with Irving, and see what he says.*

"Let me think about it, Mama. I'll get back to you."

"You're lucky to marry a man with money of his own."

"How do you know that Irving has any money?"

"He's a big spender. He gave me twice what I laid out for you to go to college," she announced with the sound of triumph in her voice.

I felt hurt by her words. It hadn't been loved, or regard for my future welfare that had prompted her to offer me the money to go to college. She'd just wanted an indentured servant to satisfy her desire for a better life.

I recalled what Daddy had said the last time I saw him, "In this life you make your own bed. So, make it a good one!"

I was glad to be able let go of the belief I'd made her life harder, or I owed her my allegiance because of what I did by squealing on my father. Mama had her money back, plus. And she was a happy woman now.

Dad had left Mama for someone who could give him a better life. Yet, I wasn't happy for my part in getting him his freedom to attain his end.

At this moment, I felt as if I were chattel traded between Mama and Irving. And I felt resentment. *Am I exchanging one yoke for another? My time in servitude with Mama is over. Is marriage supposed to be an arranged transaction?*

What does love have to do with it? What's love anyway? What will my "freedom" cost me now?

I had a sudden headache. I took two aspirins, and went to bed.

When I awoke, I was alone and felt confused, and a little frightened. I'd always lived with somebody. Was marriage the solution to my dilemma now?

I no longer felt as happy about getting married as I had been. The champagne of my life had gone flat. I didn't have to live with, or communicate with my mother, yet I didn't feel ready to live without her.

The phone rang and my heart left to hear Irving say, "I promised you I'd take care of your mother. She's agreed to our marriage. Are you ready now to set the date?"

Irving was putting me in charge of setting the date. He's willing to wait. He doesn't feel he purchased me from her. What a relief… But I wanted more time to sort out my feelings. So, I said, "Irving, my teaching contract ends in June. I don't want to commute to the Island every day after we get married."

"I don't want you to do anything you don't want to do. I can wait…but it isn't easy for me, my darling."

I was thrilled by his words, and my own increasing desires. I was confident Irving loved me. He wasn't playing games with me, or planning to hurt me. I could trust Irving. He's not like my father. And my headache vanished.

CHAPTER 40

On Sunday, Irving drove me to The Bronx to meet his mother, Annie Feller. As he drove he told me some things about her to prepare me. She was the eldest of three sisters who had come to America from Hungary.

Once she'd been considered a pretty girl. However, a terrible toothache had caused Annie to go to a dentist to stop the pain. His procedure cut a nerve, and had left her with a drooping, and scarred face.

I remembered seeing "The Hunchback of Notre Dame" and hoped she wouldn't be as deformed as Quasimodo. "The poor woman. How sad for her," I said. and was prepared for the shock of seeing a deformed face. I'd be careful to look only at her eyes.

"In the Jewish tradition the eldest daughter must be married first. So, my mother's sisters and their boyfriends got enough money together to arrange a suitable marriage for her to my father." *Aha, Irving's father was looking to land in a comfortable bed like my father had done. I guess that's what most men are like.*

Irving continued, "My father was a handsome and good man, but he had little or no business sense. He was too trusting and allowed many of his customers to run up big bills. So, Mom sent him home to take care of us boys, and she went to work in the store."

His mother was a natural businesswoman. "In no time, the grocery store was making money, and she brought in dry goods to sell in the store too.

She sent my father to do the shopping, and I went along with him to help carry the packages." *Irving was always a good and helpful son.*

"I saw that my father didn't bother to bargain down the price of goods, and I told my mother about it." *Did that make Irving a snitch also?*

"Dad was diabetic, and claimed arguing wasn't good for him. So, Mom asked me to drop out of school and help the family by doing the buying for the store. My two older brothers already worked at the store." *So, Irving, like my mother, had dropped out of school to help support his family.*

"Frankly, I didn't like school. I played hookey and smoked weed with my friends at the pool hall until I got sick. In the hospital a nurse told me smoking was unhealthy. I tried to stop, but it was too hard while my pals continued to smoke. So, I figured I'd help my parents, and I quit hanging out with my friends.

I accepted the job of buyer for the store. *Irving had on the job training. He's a smart man, and a good son.* "I'm really good at buying. We make a nice profit margin. I like being out of the store. I don't like working inside from nine to six-thirty like my brothers."

***

Irving exited from the west-side highway, and turned onto Broadway. "Since her legs got bad, Mom no longer works in the store.

She bought a two-family house for my brother Jack and his wife Betty. They live downstairs, and Mom lives upstairs. Betty looks after her."

I was glad I was going to be part of this family, and have brothers and sisters. I'd always envied my classmates who had brothers and sisters. It was very lonely being an only child, and I was looking forward to meeting my new family.

We passed Van Courtland Park. There were six soccer fields on one side, and a huge stone house and gardens beyond them. It was interesting to see the last station of the elevated IRT subway line outside my windows ended a few blocks before the Feller residence. Although we had traveled a long way from Brooklyn yet there was still a connection. I had always wondered where the subway line ended.

***

Irving parked his car on the street, and we walked a short distance to the modest two-story brick house where the Fellers lived. Irving introduced me to his sister-in-law, Betty, who met us at the door.

She was a plain looking, mature woman with a kind face, and a matronly body. Jack, his brother was taller than Irving, but not as handsome. Roger, their teenage son was a very nice looking, alert young man.

Betty said, "I'm encouraging Roger to become a baker. *Oh well, maybe he's not as bright as he looks. Don't Jewish mothers all want their sons to go to college?*

After eating our bagel and lox luncheon, Betty asked us to carry a plate of food up to her mother-in-law. I wondered why Mrs. Feller hadn't come down to have lunch with us.

We climbed the stairs, and waited several minutes before Mrs. Feller came to the door. It was painful for her to walk. She unlocked and opened the door for us.

I pitied the woman her disfigured face. She had to speak out the side of her mouth, and drooled. "Please come in and sit down in the parlor."

The Victorian furniture smelled musty, and was not particularly comfortable. She sat beside me on the couch.

"My son told me why you wanted a car instead of a diamond ring. I can see that you love him too." *Her eyes lit up whenever she looked at Irving. Did my eyes light up too?*

Mrs. Feller slipped off her diamond engagement ring and handed it to me. I admired the setting of a heart on either side of the diamond, and handed it back to her. She pushed my hand away and said, "See if it fits on your finger."

The ring did fit. Then, she astounded me by saying, "I want you should have it. I know that you'll take good care of my son."

"Oh, thank you, Mrs. Feller. "I couldn't think of anything more to say. I leaned over to kissed the cheek of the frail old woman with a faint scent of urine on her clothes.

"You may call me Annie," she said. "Please take this plate down to Betty. I don't want to give her an excuse to come up here. She's a snoop. I don't like her."

***

I returned the plate to Betty. She noticed the ring on my finger.

"That old witch has never liked me. I shop, clean, and cook for her, yet she never has a kind word for me."

"How sad she doesn't appreciate all you do for her,"

"That woman won't let me touch any of her things. She insists on putting on her own bed sheets. She claims I have a bad body odor, and she can't stand to be close to me."

"You smell okay to me. She ought to be more appreciative of all the nice things you do for her." Does *Betty get paid to do those things for her mother-in law?*

"I see the old witch must like you, Maxine. She's never given me a piece of her jewelry."

"Yes. Wasn't it nice of Annie to insist I should have an engagement ring."

"Don't ever let her hear you call her Annie. She'll bust a gut screaming at you."

I didn't mention I'd already been invited to call her Annie. *No need to make my sister-in-law more jealous of me.*

"Betty, I can't help wondering why you want Roger to become a baker."

"In my family, I learned from my mother not to expect too much from your children. Everyone did very well. So, I'm using her technique with Roger."

"What a clever idea. He'll never think he's a disappointment to you, and he'll probably do very well. I'm a teacher, and Roger impresses me as a very bright young man."

"Think so? I hope you're right. Have you met Jeffrey? He's Harry's son. He gets good grades, but I suspect he cheats."

I looked at my beautiful engagement ring. *Mama will be jealous when she sees this. And, the day I drive up in my new car she'll probably faint. I'm a lucky girl to have a car, and a ring for engagement gifts.*

Annie seems to like me. I don't foresee any trouble between us, but I think I should be wary of her. I don't want to get trapped into being her caretaker. Betty can keep that job.

Harry arrived before three o'clock. Irving introduced us. He stared brazenly at my breasts. He was leering at me as he licked his lips. I went to the bathroom to wash the hand with which I shook his.

On returning, I overheard him say, "Irving, if you have trouble getting it up, I'll be glad to do it for you." Harry reminded me of my Uncle Joe, and he didn't appear to be a helpful person.

The brothers went upstairs to visit their mother. Betty turned on her television set, and we watched a movie until the men returned.

Irving and I said our goodbyes. Harry waved and said, "See you next week," and left, also. Irving appeared upset to me, but I didn't ask him what was bothering him until we were seated in his car. "Has someone objected to something about our getting married?" *Was there going to be an unexpected obstacle as I had feared?*

"No. Why do you ask that?"

"Well, you don't look happy now."

"Mom gave me a raise, but my brothers object unless I work more hours in the store. There needs to be a change in my work schedule." *Annie doesn't work at the store anymore, yet she's the boss and calls all the shots.*

"How often is there a business meeting at your mother's place?"

"Sunday's payday. Harry lives near the store, and takes home the money each night. He brings it to Mom on Sunday. It gives her great pleasure to count up the cash the store's made. Then, she pays each of us." *Annie is lucky she can trust Harry. When cash is moved from one place to another it can be very tempting.*

"Harry could be robbed. Wouldn't it be safer for him to make nightly bank deposits?"

Irving turned to me and glared, "Mom and Pop lost a great deal of money by putting cash into a bank account back in the thirties. Mom doesn't trust banks. It would upset her a lot to ever hear you say that. Please, don't mention your ideas to my family. You know nothing about my family's business."

"Sorry, I thought I was being helpful." *He's correct. Things have been going on this way for a long time. There seems to be enough money for everyone, and they're happy, or they wouldn't still be working together. If it ain't broke, don't bother to fix it.*

CHAPTER 41

O n Monday, I was surprised to see how my fellow teachers reacted to my engagement ring. Suddenly, everyone had the time to stop and say, "Good morning, Miss Reichard". I felt accepted by them at last, and popular. *It's not always unpleasant to be the center of gossip.*

At the end of the school day on Friday, I received a note to go to the Teacher's Lounge. I opened the door and was greeted by decorations and signs saying, "Good Luck," and "He's a Lucky Fellow." It was a delightful surprise. Their joy at my happiness brought tears to my eyes. *These strangers cared more about me than my own family did.*

The following week, Mr. Marasa, the principal, sent for me. "I understand that you're getting married Miss Reichard.

"Yes, sir."

"Are you planning to teach in Lindenhurst next year?"

"I'm sorry to say, no. The commute from the City is just too far. I've enjoyed working here. I'll miss you all."

"Well, we're sorry to lose you. You did a good job here for us, and the children." He smiled and said, "Good luck on your next job. Would you like me to write you a letter of recommendation?"

"Thank you, sir. That would be very nice of you."

CHAPTER 42

My driving instructor drove me to take the driving test. One of the ladies waiting there told me she'd failed it twice. That made me feel nervous. *What good is a car if I can't drive it?*

The man who was to give me the test scowled. I had butterflies in my stomach. I made sure to signal before I pulled out. I used hand signals making my turns. He used his pencil to check off whatever I did on his sheet.

All seemed to be going well until we reached a narrow street with a garbage truck blocking the road. *Oy vey.* The driver signaled me to pass him. *Is there enough space?*

I managed to pass the truck without any mishap, and the tester said, "That's it. Go back to the starting point, and park." *I've failed this test. He's had enough of my bad driving.*

***

Irving phoned to ask me how the test went.

"I think I failed."

"I'm sure you passed. What color car would you like?"

"Blue is my favorite."

"What make?"

"I don't know anything about the makes of cars. Whatever you pick out for me will be just fine."

"I think you'll like the new Pontiac."

"Sounds fine to me, but shouldn't you wait and see if I passed the test?"

"I'll order it now. By the time it gets here you'll have your driving license."

"Well, I hope you know a good place to keep it parked until I can drive it."

Why is he laughing? Doesn't he understand I'm worried about failing?

Several days later there was a letter from the Motor Vehicle people. To my surprise and relief it said I'd passed.

Wow. *I did it on my first try.* Irving's faith in me wasn't misplaced, and it renewed my confidence in my abilities. *He may know me better than I do.* Feeling better about myself, I was able to think about our wedding date.

***

We went to see the ballet "Swan Lake" on Saturday night. As we drove home I asked, "Are you sure that you want to marry me, Irving?"

He pulled over and parked. Then he took me in his arms and covered me with warm, moist kisses. His hand wandered to my breast, and I didn't push it away this time.

"We can fly to Las Vegas and get married tonight," he said.

"It wouldn't be fair to our families not to have them present at our wedding. Mama offered to pay for it if I didn't invite my father. What do you think about that?"

"What do you think about it?"

"I should be free to invite whomever I want."

"You tell her just that. We can afford to pay for our own wedding. Don't let anyone lay down conditions on my Maxine."

Irving doesn't want me as his indentured servant. He wants me to be his queen.

On Sunday, Irving and I went to see Annie. I drove us in my new car. She was at the door to greet us when we arrived. She handed me a neatly wrapped box and said it was a wedding gift to take care of Irving.

It was very light. Nothing rattled inside. I didn't try to peek inside. *Does Annie have all her marbles? I guess it's the thought that really counts.*

I had a hunch Annie wanted to speak in private with her son. So, I went to my car to put the gift in the trunk. I was parked two blocks away.

On my way back, I noticed a "For Sale" sign on a house similar to the one where Jack and Betty lived several doors down.

I climbed the steps at Annie's, and Irving met me at the door. "Please put this box in the car also," I figured the old lady was a bit touched to be giving us another present. *It's sweet she wants to be thought of as a generous woman.*

The day was pleasant, and I didn't mind taking another walk. I returned to the house in time to greet Harry as he parked his Chevrolet.

Millie, his wife, had come with him this time. She was about my height but much thinner and looked many years older than me. She had a sharp, shrewish face, and a voice to match.

She didn't smile when I extended my hand which was accepted limply. *I'll bet she has Harry under her thumb.*

In the house, Harry went upstairs with a brown paper shopping bag. Jack left his apartment and climbed the stairs, also. Millie walked to Betty's door, and I followed her inside. Millie said, "I can smell the cat litter, Betty."

"I don't have a cat anymore. If I'd known you were coming I'd have put some out for you."

Wow. These women don't act like the loving sister-in-law I'd hoped to have.

I said, "Betty, I've been admiring your kitchen curtains. Are they new?" "She only changes them for Passover," Millie said.

"Oh, do you keep a kosher house, Betty?"

"Well, at least I try to do it."

Millie asked, "What do you mean by that crack?"

"Your home reeks from bacon. Air Wick doesn't do as good a job as you think."

"Betty, you're a snoop just like the old lady says."

I'd had *enough of this nonsense, and* I took refuge in the bathroom. My dream of having a loving family was fading as I overheard those two cats squabble over nothing.

I flushed the toilet to let them know that I was about to return. Betty, at least, tried to be agreeable. But that Millie… *What was she like before Harry married her? Does she have something nice about her besides her body? Maybe, I was blessed to be an only child.*

I asked, "Can you ladies play gin rummy?" They shook their heads.

"Casino, or Steal the Old Man's Bundle?"

Betty snickered, "Millie should be good at that one."

I asked, "Were you a bookkeeper, Millie?"

Before she answered, the door opened and the men returned. "Time to leave."

***

Irving and I walked to my car. Whew… I felt glad to be out of there.

"My mother really likes you a lot. After we get married she wants to buy us a house." *Uh oh. I bet it's the one I saw for sale down the street.*

"Irving, dear, that's so sweet of her, but until I know which school I'm going to be teaching at … it just isn't a good idea yet."

"Oh, you're planning to continue teaching after we get married?"

"Yes it's why I went to college. I love teaching. It's such a rewarding job. I'm planning to teach until I get pregnant."

"I like that idea. You're a smart girl just like Mom says."

"Annie's very sweet. I like her too." *Whew. I'm glad I headed him off before he went any further.*

I drove us to the apartment in Brooklyn. I had suggested to Irving he leave his car in front of my house. Then, after I had driven to The Bronx. It gave him time to relax driving from Manhattan, and it kept my parking place waiting for me when we got back.

"Irving, I'm going to discuss our wedding with my mother as soon as we get back to Brooklyn."

"Can you handle her, or do you want me there to back you up?"

"Knowing I have alternatives available to me, I doubt that I'll have trouble with her. It'll be okay."

"In that case, I'll leave as soon as we get to your place. It'll be easier for me to find a parking spot on Riverside Drive at this time of day." Irving kissed me goodbye, got into his car, and drove away.

I parked, and went up the concrete stoop to the front door. Aunt Jean was sitting on the statue of the lion.

She said, "It's not nice to kiss in public."

"It's a lot nicer than you asking me to help you to steal from my employer when I was a kid working at the five and dime store."

She turned crimson, and hurried inside. I had wanted to say that to her for a very long time, but feared the consequences from my mother. *Wow. It's great to be free to speak my mind. I'm glad I'm no longer the little kid others feel free to push around. Now, I needn't be scared if Mama yells, and tells me to get out. I have a car, a place to go, and someone who loves me.*

I walked upstairs and unlocked the door. "Hi Mama," I said. "Let's go into the living room and talk about my wedding."

"What's gotten into you lately. You used to be such a sweet child."

"Let's talk about the wedding. You said you wanted to pay for it?"

"Only if you don't invite your father."

"Mama, I've thought it over. It's my wedding, and I have to be free to invite anyone I choose.'

Mama gave me a wary look, but didn't yell at me. I sensed the wheels in her head were turning as she realized I wasn't afraid of her any longer.

"Well, I can understand it might be embarrassing if your father wasn't present at your wedding."

"You're 100% correct. You're a clever woman. It's not that I care whether or not he comes. You'll be the one who walks me down the aisle to give me away. You're the parent who supported me when I was young. I know you did the best you could. It's time for us to let go of anger about the past and forgive one another."

She looked me in the eye and smiled. "Yes, it is," she said.

CHAPTER 43

Mama phoned me in Lindenhurst to tell me all the caterers she'd contacted were booked, and so were the synagogues. I wondered if she was trying to stall my wedding?

"Thanks for trying, Mama. Don't worry. I'll find us a place. *We can always get married at the Court House.*"

***

I phoned Rabbi Cohen, a neighbor who lived in the building next to a friend of mine in Brooklyn. "Rabbi, time is short and I need to get married right away."

"Maxine, you were always a good and polite child. Is this man Jewish?"

"Yes."

"Then, I'll marry you in my study. Let me check my appointment calendar and I'll give you the date… Let's see … I have a wedding scheduled for 12:30 on June twelfth. So, I can marry you at 10:30 AM. Please be sure not to be late. Wedding guests often come earlier."

"Fine. What's the address? How many people may attend?" "The room seats fifty," he laughed.

"Thank you, Rabbi Cohen. We'll see you on the twelfth. Thank you."

***

Irving had taken me for dinner and dancing at The Boulevard restaurant on Queens Boulevard earlier that year. The place would be convenient for our guests from either Brooklyn, The Bronx, or Manhattan. It was ideal. I prayed, then phoned the restaurant.

The man who answered chuckled when I told him we wanted to reserve June twelfth for our wedding reception. "If you don't mind the service will be slow on that date, I'll be happy to accommodate you." "Great."

"You'll have to use the upstairs dining room. The entrance is at the top of the wooden staircase on the side of the building."

"Do you need a deposit now?'

"It's customary to put down ten percent of the overall bill. How soon can you get it here?"

"My fiancé will pay you before Saturday." I phoned Irving and told him about the arrangements I'd made. And that we had to get a deposit to the restaurant as soon as possible.

"I'll give it to him tomorrow. Ha-ha! he laughed. Wait 'til I tell Harry you've arranged everything. Mollie said we wouldn't be able to get married before September. I'm so proud of you, my darling Maxine. I love you."

"I love you, Irving." It was the first time I'd allowed myself to say it. Before then, I suspected it might be my eagerness to get away from Mama, or the fear of becoming an old maid, as Grandma had predicted, or both, prompting me to say "yes" to Irving.

CHAPTER 44

Irving slept in my mother's front bedroom the night before our wedding. My girlfriend Florence was giving us our Wedding Album as a gift. Her father was a retired professional photographer.

His studio was now in the basement of his home on Shore Parkway. We were to drive there before the ceremony at the rabbi's studio. We planned on arriving at 8:00 AM It would give us plenty of time to pose for pictures, and still be able to get to the rabbi by 10:30 AM.

***

However, after the photo shoot, we ran into a traffic standstill.

"There must be an accident," Irving said. "No telling how long it'll take to clear it. I'd better go back another way."

Irving drove for miles guessing how to go. He kept running into unanticipated construction, and repeatedly had to take detours. We passed no open gasoline stations.

Finally, he pulled over to a curb and sobbed, "I'm sorry, Maxine, but I'm lost."

***

I saw a police car and waved it down.

Irving asked, "What're you doing?"

"Getting us help."

"From a policeman?"

The police car stopped, and the red-haired, freckle-faced cop walked up to us.

"Officer, we're lost," I said. "We're supposed to get married at 10:30 on Eastern Parkway."

"Congratulations. Just follow me and I'll put you on the right street to get you there."

The policeman got back into his car, and with his siren blaring through the side streets and red lights to the end of his district. He waved and pointed to the way we needed to go to get to our destination. It was now 10:05 AM.

Irving said, "I never thought a policeman would be helpful to me."

En route to the rabbi's studio we hit another traffic jam. It appeared a driver had swerved to avoid running into barrels which had fallen off a truck, and he'd crashed into the traffic light at the intersection, and broken it. Traffic was stalled in all directions, and no policeman was in sight.

I said, "The rabbi is doing me a big favor. He asked that we not be late. What can we do?"

It was 10:20 AM. Irving drove slowly onto the sidewalk of Eastern Parkway. *"If we get arrested, we won't have time to get married."* I was scared. People jumped out of our way waving their fists, and cursing at us.

***

We reached Eastern Parkway and Nostrand Avenue where traffic was moving at a normal pace. Irving got back onto the street without any mishap. *Whew.*

***

We reached the address on Eastern Parkway the Rabbi had given me. The cars of my friends were parked along the street. No space was left for us. Irving said, "I'll have to double-park,"

***

We hurried into the building at ten fifty-five and were greeted with applause and cheers from our guests. Someone voiced the fear that we'd chickened out. Rabbi Cohen wiped his brow. He motioned to us to get under the Chupa where he would perform the ceremony.

Mama stood next to it wearing a white brocade dress. *So that's the dress she'd told me she'd bought. Doesn't she know only the bride is supposed to wear white?* Irving's brothers and wives had brought several bottles of wine. Sliced honey cake and sponge cakes were laid out on a side table.

The study was decorated with flowers for the noon wedding. The fragrance of the beautiful white gladioli, mums, and gardenias was overpowering. I felt dizzy. Everything seemed to fade into a distant blur. The room became a giant soup bowl, and I was standing in the middle of it.

Irving already stood beneath the marriage canopy. *Have I made the right decision? This is for keeps.* I was trembling and unable to move. I heard whispering in the distance. Then, Irving came to get me. He took my arm, and supported me as we walked up the white aisle runner to the waiting Rabbi.

He started to chant the wedding prayers in Hebrew. This wasn't a language I understood. We went through the motions, and exchanged rings when the Rabbi directed us. Irving smashed a wine glass under his shoe, and it was over. *Despite your awful prediction Grandma, I'm a married woman.* A flood of relief and joy washed over me replacing my worries and fear. I had no doubts. I'd married the man I loved and trusted.

After the ceremony, a flood of relief coursed through me. I was energized and overjoyed to be holding the hand of my beloved husband. I knew I'd done the right thing.

I looked around the room to see who had come. My dad was there. Blanche hadn't come with him. *Was she afraid to give Mama the opportunity to confront her for stealing her husband, and being the other woman? My big sister Selma had come.* It was amusing to overhear Mama boast to my dad she'd arranged the wedding and the flowers.

I was happy my sister Selma was there. She hugged me, and whispered a warning, "Carry nothing that you'll be sorry to lose in your purse tonight."

"Okay. I'll just take my lipstick and a comb."

Selma introduced me to her companion, Zachery Klett. I'd heard a rumor she was living with a man. Selma had once told me she had no intention of marrying "a pig in a poke." She never wanted to be divorced either.

Zach had an intelligent look about him. He was slender, tall, and had clear, bright blue eyes. He didn't look Jewish. He was a chain smoker, and I didn't like that about him. I wondered if Selma would become one, too.

***

I walked over to Annie and kissed and hugged her, and all my new in-laws. These people were now my family. I hoped I would be able to get them to behave more civilly toward one another.

***

I had no desire to see anyone in my real family after today. They had never treated me with loving respect while I was grew up. Good riddance to them… except for Mama. I thought she was a bright woman who would've been very different if Grandma hadn't pulled her out of school. Now, she had some money. She could learn to be a bookkeeper. It would pay far better than a bakery saleswoman receives. I thought she'd use some of the money Irving had given to her to better her life.

***

Irving announced that the reception would be at The Boulevard restaurant located on Queens Boulevard. He invited everyone to come. There'd been no time to have directions to the restaurant printed.

The scheduled noon wedding party was due to arrive, and the Rabbi came to congratulate us, and hurry us out. Irving handed him a one-hundred-dollar bill. He was surprised and smiled.

***

Time to throw my bridal bouquet. The single ladies assembled at the foot of the stairs. I removed the orchid corsage, and handed it to Mama. Then, I turned my back to the women and threw the bouquet over my head. The girlfriend of Irving's friend, Barney, caught it. I was glad for them and wished them well.

***

Mama smiled and pinned the corsage on me, and not her own dress. She got that right.

I was glad I'd selected a simple, white silk crepe, Grecian-styled dress. And as we left, I thought, *Lord, thank you for all these lovely flowers at our wedding.*

My friends had hung a "Just Married" sign on our car, and tied a string of cans to it. I was relieved we hadn't gotten a ticket for double parking.

At the traffic light, Irving removed the noisy cans.

We raced to the restaurant intent on getting a legal parking space before our guests took them all.

CHAPTER 45

We were surprised by how crowded the restaurant parking lot was on a Sunday afternoon. Luckily, someone pulled out just as we arrived. Irving took that space.

Irving said, "I ordered everyone chicken dinners. I hope the service is slow. Our guests will need time to search the neighborhood for a parking space."

We climbed up the wooden stairs to the dining room. The flowers had arrived, but no one had placed them on the tables. Irving and I rushed to put out the floral centerpieces in place.

The band arrived, unpacked their instruments and started playing in the empty room. Two by two the wedding guests started to enter. Soon the floor was crowded with dancing couples.

My tummy rumbled. *Our guests must be hungry too.* "Irving dear, I was told the food service would be slow in coming, but this is ridiculous."

"I'll go see what's the matter."

"I'm coming with you. I'm not staying here to apologize for poor service." We left the banquet room. From the top of the stairs we were astonished to see chicken dinners strewn all over the steps, and on the ground below. At least twenty dogs happily wagging their tails, and a dozen cats were enjoying our wedding dinners.

The sight looked so absurd to me I burst out laughing. I thought if it were true kindness to animals brings good luck, then we were going to be very lucky indeed.

"Irving, this is a good omen."

"What?" He scowled. "How can you say that? This is one awful mess."

Stepping carefully to avoid the dinners littering the stairs we went into the main restaurant to complain to the person in charge. A waiter directed us to the owner who was sitting at the center of a banquet table with then the food and dishes went flying everywhere.

"New dinners have already been prepared for you, and will be served shortly."

After telling us that he introduced us to the bride, his daughter and new son-in-law. We congratulated one another. They invited us to stay and have a steak dinner with them. We were very hungry and tempted, but declined their kind offer.

"We must return to our wedding guests."

The owner said, "I apologize for this great inconvenience, Mr. and Mrs. Feller. So, I'm going to forget about the balance of your bill." Irving shook his hand, and we left the restaurant.

"Maxine, I have to apologize to you. I thought you were nutty to say the mess we saw was a good luck omen, but you were right. My deposit was ten percent of the bill, and now it has paid for our whole wedding feast."

He kissed me. "Darling," he said, "we've saved a lot of money today." *Ah, kindness to animals does bring good luck.*

"We can go to Las Vegas for a real honeymoon, after we spend tonight at Number One Fifth Avenue. I've a hunch we're on a lucky streak. I want to play it to the end."

"Sounds exciting. How will we get there?"

"Why, we'll fly of course."

"Fly? Err-r, Irving, I've never flown in a plane."

"Don't be nervous. I'll hold your hand all the way."

We returned to our hungry wedding guests, and Irving announced dinner was on its way. They all cheered. Then, he told them what had happened. Annoyance and grumbling soon changed to laughter.

Uncle Joe did a Russian kizatski dance for our guests. When he finished he caught his breath, and said "You was always my favorite niece, Maxine. I wish you naches." I thought lucky me, *I bet that'll be his only gift.*

"Thank you, Uncle Joe. I enjoyed your dance."

"Whew! It's the last time I'll ever do it. I'm getting too old for that kind of mishegaas."

Looking at my relatives around the room, I realized how much everyone had aged since I'd last seen them. *The next time we meet will probably be at another wedding, or a funeral… maybe theirs.*

CHAPTER 46

Our bags were in the trunk of Irving's car. There was no reason for us to return to Brooklyn. We drove straight to Number One Fifth Avenue where Irving had made a reservation for our wedding night.

Irving registered and got the key to our room from the desk clerk. We'd brought no luggage, so we didn't need a bellman, and took the elevator alone.

Irving inserted the key and pushed open the door. He picked me up and carried me over the threshold. "I'm taking you to bed."

Inside we were surprised to find that our room wasn't just a bedroom. It was a suite of rooms. Irving insisted on carrying me to bed. But first he had to find the bedroom.

One door led to a kitchen, another to a library, and another to a huge closet. Finally, Irving opened the door to the bedroom. He put me on the bed. Ater carrying me around, I hoped he wasn't exhausted.

He removed his boutonnière and tossed it over his shoulder. We heard a loud ping as it landed into the metal waste paper basket. We laughed at his lucky shot.

Irving was undressed before I'd removed my stockings. He had an erection as he watched me remove my dress and undies. I'd never undressed in front of a man, and I quickly got under the covers.

"Don't be embarrassed. You have a beautiful body. I've never touched anyone as soft. Your skin feels like rose petals." He drew me closer to him, and I enjoyed the warmth of his body and his moist kisses.

***

In the morning, I was surprised when I couldn't find my purse. I was glad to have heeded Selma's warning. Irving gave me money to buy a new lipstick and a comb in the lobby.

"This place is very nice, Irving. We won't require more than a one-bedroom apartment for now. I could easily live here."

"I know that you'll find us a nice place to live. Are you ready to go to the airport?"

"I guess so."

***

When we left our hotel, I noticed the Brevoort Hotel, across the street, was building condominium apartments next to it. "Wouldn't that be a nice place for us to live, Irving?"

"It's a very nice neighborhood, but too far downtown for me to commute to the store." *Probably too expensive too.* "I've heard Scarsdale in Westchester is a nice area for newlyweds. It'd be much easier for me to go to work from there."

"You're right, dear. When we get back, I'll find us a place close to the store."

"You're trembling, Maxine. I can see you're really worried about flying."

"Yes."

"Hold my hand. I know you're going to love it once you get used to it. It's sort of like sex."

I giggled. "That's encouraging, and reassuring." I took his hand and he drove to La Guardia Airport.

Irving purchased two round-trip tickets to Las Vegas. We walked out of the terminal, across the tarmac, to climb the stairs to board the plane. He told the stewardess that this was my first flight. She smiled and offered me a small package of "Chicklets" gum before showing me how to buckle the seat belt.

***

The plane shook as the motors roared and the propellers rotated. I saw flames spurting out of one of the engines and told Irving it was on fire. Irving assured me it wasn't. The aircraft taxied into takeoff position. It vibrated and rattled loudly as we sped along the runway. After we left the ground it was suddenly very quiet.

I looked out the window. We were in the air. I squeezed Irving's hand, and he smiled. I was relieved that I hadn't wet my panties.

It was fascinating to see the buildings below as the plane climbed higher and higher. Soon, white fluffy clouds were below us. *Wow. Birds don't fly this high.*

125

Irving said, "I phoned to book us into the Sand's Hotel. We'll be seeing Frank Sinatra performing there." I was thrilled. I'd never dreamt life could be this exciting.

The stewardess served us a light dinner, and a bottle of champagne. Stars appeared in the blue velvet sky. I soon fell asleep on my husband's shoulder.

The voice of the pilot announcing we were about to land in Las Vegas awakened me. I kissed Irving and put on my seat belt.

He held my hand during the landing. Taking off had been exciting, but I was frightened as we came closer and closer to the ground. I remembered my Uncle Al who had bought a plane with his mustering out pay from the army crashed into something every time he landed. Segrum, his Icelandic wife, insisted he sell it before he got seriously hurt, and he did.

***

Our plane bumped when the wheels touched the ground, and bounced a few times before it came to a halt. We were down without crashing. I realized a well- trained pilot didn't crash whenever he landed.

***

We walked into the terminal to claim our luggage. I noticed rows of strange looking machines around the airport. Several of our fellow passengers were putting nickels or quarters into them while we waited for the bags to arrive.

One lady started jumping up and down as a flood of nickels tumbled out of the machine she'd been feeding. I helped her to pick them up from the floor. She surprised me when she handed one back to me and said, "Dearie, keep this one for luck."

I didn't have a purse, or a pocket, and I slipped it into my bra.

***

Irving collected our luggage, and we walked outside. The hotel had sent a car to meet its guests. *What nice treatment. I felt like we were celebrities.* We arrived at the hotel and Irving went to the desk to register.

In the center of the gold-painted, and cream-colored marble lobby was a gold colored, carpeted restaurant. I recognized Frank Sinatra having dinner with several men at the table. Wow.

A bellboy led us to the elevator and up to our room. I unpacked while Irving showered and shaved. It was a nice room, but not as nice as our Number One Fifth Avenue suite. When Irving was finished, then I took my shower.

Coming out of the bathroom door, I was surprised to see Irving dressed and ready to leave the room. "Aren't we going to bed?"

"No. Get dressed. The evening has just begun here in Vegas. Would you like to see a movie, or gamble?"

"My hair is a mess. I was going to the hairdresser tomorrow."

Irving picked up the phone and made an appointment for me at the beauty shop in the lobby in an hour. I was surprised. "Are they open this late?"

"Las Vegas is a city that never sleeps. I'll gamble while I wait for you to get your hair done. After that, would you like to go to a movie?"

"Okay."

Irving showed me where in the noisy Casino I could find him after my hair appointment. We stopped at a caged window and he traded some cash for chips. He gave me his cash to hold, and several chips I could use when I returned. I kissed him and left to search for the beauty shop.

***

It was next to an elegant dress shop. I gawked at the exquisite dresses in the window, but didn't bother to go inside to price them. I was certain they were too expensive.

My beautician talked me into getting a chic new style haircut, and applied a variety of products to my face hoping I would buy them. I did purchase a lipstick and moisturizer with suntan lotion in it.

***

Afterward, I went to find Irving. I spotted him at one of the craps tables, and stood beside him. He didn't comment on how nice I looked. "I'm not ready to leave yet," he said.

I saw the "odds" displayed on the crap table. "Any Craps" paid thirty-three to one. I thought that was worth the gamble of one of my chips. Irving placed one of his chips on the pass line, and I placed one of mine on "Any Craps". I won! I collected my chips and continued to stand next to Irving.

He placed a chip on "The Field" and won. He grinned, "Wow. You're bringing me luck."

"Are you ready to go now?"

"Not yet. I want to win back some of the money I lost."

He played the field and won again. Then, it was his turn to roll the dice. He placed several chips on the Pass line and rolled a seven and was paid. He left the chips there and rolled a six. No one paid Irving, but they didn't take away his chips. He told me he had to roll a six again.

He rolled a four, and then a five. I crossed my fingers and hoped for a six but he rolled a seven, and they took away his chips. Irving was disappointed, and so was I.

It was my turn to roll. I put five chips on "Any Craps" closed my eyes and tossed the dice. A seven came up and I lost my bet. However, Irving had placed all his chips on the pass line, and he won.

"Let's go," I said. I didn't like the feeling of losing my chips.

"Roll again," he said.

I didn't place a bet and rolled a seven. *This game is a waste of time and money.* I rolled and made another seven.

I said, "It looks to me like you've won back more than you started out with. Let's go now."

The people around the table groaned because I wanted to leave. Irving put most of his chips into his pocket and asked me to roll again. I was annoyed by his request and wanted to demonstrate it to him. I removed my original investment chips from my winnings and placed the rest on "Any Craps", and I won.

Now, Irving agreed it was time for us to leave.

We cashed in our chips. Our winnings went into the vault in our room. We didn't bother to count it. Irving talked about playing again tomorrow. I yawned.

"Las Vegas doesn't need to sleep, but I do. I'm going to bed now."

***

I awoke later to go to the bathroom., Irving was gone. I checked the vault. He'd taken a lot of the money that we'd won. I removed the money I'd won. These were my winnings. I put them in the new purse I'd bought at the dress shop before we came upstairs. I was dozing off when Irving returned. He went to the vault and got out more money.

"Honey, please come to bed," I said. "You need your rest."

"I lost a lot of money. My luck is bound to turn if I keep on playing."

"Okay, but please don't take more than half of what's in there." "I won't."

***

When I awoke in the morning, Irving lay asleep on the bed fully dressed. I removed his shoes. He looked exhausted. I checked the vault and saw that some money was still in there. *This place isn't a wholesome environment for us. After we hear Sinatra, I'm going to suggest we go home.*

Irving had mentioned there was a complimentary breakfast in the lobby. I left him asleep, and went downstairs to get us some food.

In the lobby, I saw a sign announcing the sale of Las Vegas City acreage starting at forty-five dollars an acre. It would begin at noon. Returning to the room with the food, I mentioned this to Irving when he awoke.

***

"Forty-five dollars an acre for sand? Are you nuts!"

"Well, I thought I'd frame the real estate certificate. It would be nice to have it as a souvenir reminding us of our honeymoon in Las Vegas."

"No. I refuse to permit you to throw our money away on real estate that's sand."

"Okay." *He'd rather toss it away playing dice.* I hoped he didn't plan on gambling in New York City too. I'd heard it said, "All gamblers die broke." I had no intention of letting that happen to us.

CHAPTER 47

We returned to New York, and went to Irving's place on Riverside Drive. I learned then it wasn't his apartment. He was renting a bedroom from a Mrs. Smith, an attractive widow. She frowned on seeing me with Irving. She stared at the rings on my finger.

She said to Irving, "I rented you a room because you told me that you were a bachelor. Since you're no longer single, you'll have to move out."

Seeing his face become red and his mouth open and close without speaking, I figured Irving was embarrassed, and at a loss for words. "My husband has spoken very highly of you, Mrs. Smith. We'll be getting another place to live as soon as possible."

"Good."

***

In the morning, Irving drove his car to work. I took the subway to Brooklyn to get my car. I'd parked it in front of my mother's building. I bought a Scarsdale newspaper at a stand before I got on the train, and read the rental ads. I circled two that looked interesting.

***

At my mother's apartment, I telephoned and learned one place had already been rented. I phoned for an appointment to see the other. It was still available. I drove there immediately.

I hoped to rent the eighty-five dollar-a-month apartment as soon as it was shown to me, but the island-kitchen was in the middle of the living room. *It will smell up the entire apartment if I burnt any food. This isn't the apartment for a bride like me.*

Disappointed, I sat in my car rubbing the Geronimo Indian head on my steering wheel, and I wished I could find a good place for us to live.

***

I was unable to go back the way I'd come because of the highway construction. Then, I encountered a series of detours. I found myself on the Henry Hudson Parkway and admired the tall residential buildings on either side. *Maybe I can find an apartment in one of these buildings.*

I exited at 246th Street and tried to stay on the service road, but, again due to construction, I was forced to go up a hill before I could turn around. There were two apartment buildings along this road. I pulled up to the first one and asked the doorman if there were any apartments for rent.

"Go see Joe. He's the doorman in the next building. He mentioned to me someone was looking to sublease."

After that, I parked at the curb, and went inside to wait for Joe in the tastefully decorated lobby adorned with American Indian artifacts. *My Pontiac would be happy to live here.* Soon, a short-uniformed man carrying a plunger got off the elevator.

"You must be Joe. I was told that you're a very helpful fellow."

He laughed. "I try."

"I heard there's a sublease available here."

***

We took the elevator to the seventh floor. He used a passkey to unlock the apartment. A Pullman kitchen was in front of us. It had a door on both ends. *Thank goodness.* The living room was L-shaped with a wall of windows facing a beautiful meditation wall. The bedroom had a dusty-rose-colored papered ceiling adorned with white orchids and gold etched roses. *Wow. I like this apartment, but I bet it's expensive.*

"Very nice. How much is the rent?"

"It's a hundred-twenty-five dollars a month, but that includes gas and electricity and a garage space."

Hmm. Irving's paying forty-five for one bedroom and must hunt for parking, and we need to get out of there right away. Maybe he'll agree to take this place. I hope so.

"My husband will have to see it and approve before I can say yes."

He grinned, "I like to see a wife who listens to her husband, and respects him. I won't show it to anyone else until he sees it."

"Thank you. What's the address here?"

"Forty-five twenty-five, Henry Hudson Parkway, Riverdale. That's the West Bronx." Then he told me how to get back to Manhattan using the West Side Highway.

***

After I paid the ten-cent toll on the Henry Hudson Bridge, I was awed at the view of the George Washington Bridge. *Wow! It'll be great for Irving to see this site every morning on his way to work.*

***

With difficulty I found a parking space on Riverside Drive. I walked several blocks to Mrs. Smith's apartment. I took the elevator to the third floor.

In the hallway I could hear a woman inside an apartment yelling at someone. I grew up with my parents screaming at each other, and then Yetta and "Mama" screaming back and forth. I wouldn't tolerate anyone who screamed.

I rapped on the door. The noise stopped. *Has Mrs. Smith been yelling at my husband?* She answered the door. I saw that Irving looked upset. *Why hadn't he told her off?*

I said, "Sweetheart, I've got good news. I think I've found us a place to live, but you have to approve it first."

Irving relaxed on hearing this. "See, Mrs. Smith, I'm not trying to take advantage of your good nature, and I refuse to give you more money for my room."

What luck. He doesn't want to stay here. He might be willing to pay one hundred-twenty-five dollars a month to get out of here.

We left Mrs. Smith's and went to dinner at the Tip Top restaurant on Broadway. I told him, "The apartment in Scarsdale wasn't suitable."

"But, you said you found a place for me to look at."

"As it happens, there was highway construction when I left Scarsdale, and I got lost coming home. I wound up in Riverdale, and found us a lovely sublease apartment. It costs a little more than the one in Scarsdale but it has

132

a garage space included in the rent. So, when you come home tired after work you won't have to hunt for a place to park."

"I like that."

"I thought you would. Also, gas and electricity are included in the rent."

"It sounds like it's going to be more than one-hundred dollars."

"Wait until you see it, Irving. There's a fabulous view of a beautiful forest, and you can see the Hudson River from the living room windows."

"Uh-oh, that sounds like a lot more than a hundred dollars. I don't think we can afford it. How much is it?"

"Honey, let's go see the apartment before you make up your mind. It's right next to the highway, and less than fifteen minutes from 125th Street."

"Oh?"

"Until I get my teaching job, I'll help you sell merchandise at the store."

"Oh? Well, it's only fair that I look at it after you went through all that trouble to find it."

A high rental will discourage Irving from thinking he can afford to gamble. I hope he likes it. How could anyone not like it?

CHAPTER 48

The next morning, we drove to Riverdale to see the apartment. Joe wasn't on duty. The day doorman knew nothing about the sublease. I asked to see the rental agent. He fetched Rudy, the superintendent.

"We're Mr. and Mrs. Feller. I know apartment 701 is available for sublease. I brought my husband to see it before we decide whether or not to rent it."

Rudy led us to the apartment and unlocked the door. *Wow The place looked even better in full daylight.* Irving smiled as he walked to the windows and admired the view of the river. His jaw dropped when he saw the bedroom. He liked it too.

Rudy said, "The price is $150 per month."

I said, "Oh, we'll only need one garage space, Rudy. I was told that thet rent was $125."

"Oh, I didn't know that you knew that. Well, the apartment is listed at that price. Er-r, you're right, Mrs. Feller. The former tenant did have two cars." "When can we move in?" Irving asked.

"A two months deposit is required, and you'll need to sign a lease."

To my surprise and Rudy's, Irving withdrew a wad of cash from his pocket and counted out the required amount. He said, "I have some furniture in storage. I'll need to notify them to bring my things here. When can we move in?"

What? I'm supposed to start out my married life with another woman's furniture? Hmm. I won't object now. Irving's willing to rent the apartment. Later on I'll dispose of anything I don't like. First things first.

"You can move in tomorrow, Mr. Feller. I should have realized you must be friends with Mr. Fisher who built and owns these buildings."

Irving didn't bother to reply. We followed Rudy to the rental agent's office where Irving signed the lease. Rudy handed me a copy along with the keys. "We have to go to work now, Maxine."

"Our luggage is in the trunk of the car. Wouldn't it be a good idea to leave it in our apartment?"

Rudy said, "If you're in a hurry, Mr. Feller, the doorman can keep it locked up in the lobby."

"Here's two dollars, Rudy. Please, have him take it to my apartment."

After Irving paid the Henry Hudson bridge toll, I said, "Wait 'til you see the

George Washington bridge around the next curve."

He took in the view. "Very nice. You've found us a good place to live."

"We accomplished a lot this morning, I couldn't wait to see the store." *If he carries all that money in his pocket, Irving must be rich. I wonder if Feller's Department Store is a big place?*

CHAPTER 49

Irving parked the car on Amsterdam Avenue, and we walked to 125th Street. A large yellow sign with red letters proclaiming "Feller's Department Store" hung over the double-windowed dry goods store. I was disappointed but said nothing. It wasn't even as large as the F. W. Woolworth five-and-ten-cent store where I'd once worked.

The store was crowded with customers. Merchandise filled shelves that climbed the walls to a tin-tiled ceiling. Harry shouted, "It's about time you got here, little brother. Get to work." He didn't even bother to say, "Good morning," to me.

Irving showed me where to put my purse in the rear of the store then left to wait on the customers. Back here and in the basement, merchandise was stacked without rhyme or reason. *How can anyone find anything in this disorganized place?*

I went to the front of the store and stood behind one of the two counters. I familiarized myself with what was for sale there.

The black saleswoman said, "Miss, customers can't come behind the counter."

"I'm Irving's wife. I'm here to sell, too."

"Oh, you're Maxine. I'm Ann. This is the ladies wear counter."

At the crowded counter she continued to wait on customers. After a few minutes of reconnoitering, I was able to help her.

***

At one o'clock, Irving came for me, and we walked to a very nice restaurant a few blocks away. *Ah, the air feels so good after being cooped up all day*

"Sweetheart," I said, "when we get back, please turn on the air conditioner. It's much too stuffy in there."

"We don't have one."

"What do you do when the weather gets hot?"

"We sweat a lot."

"It's a wonder that your customers don't go elsewhere to shop."

"They know we give them the best value for their dollar. Even when they move out of the neighborhood, they come back to do their shopping with us."

"It's great that you give good deals, but wouldn't it be a healthier place for people to shop if you put in an air conditioner?"

***

Later in the afternoon, a grossly overweight woman asked Ann to show her a dress in a size ten. Ann went into the back, returned, and showed the woman a dress in her size, yet marked size ten.

After the sale was rung up on the register, the woman left smiling. I said to Ann, "That dress couldn't have been a size ten."

She laughed, "I keep the customers happy, and hold onto my job. If she wants to see a size ten tag on her dress then I switch the tag in the back. I bring her what she asks for." *Hmm. Give the customers what they want.*

***

Harry became upset when the store was out of stock on an item. He screamed at Irving, "It's your fault we lost sales today. Why didn't you replace the stock? You're not doing a very good job."

Irving hung his head and looked anxious. He got red in the face, but said nothing in reply to his brother.

I said, "Harry, Irving should shop in the morning, and then come to work, or you'll be losing more sales." Harry glared at me and said nothing yet continued to berate Irving.

I noticed that Harry shoved into his pockets the cash from the big sales he made. *Wasn't he supposed to ring up all sales on the cash register?*

***

As we drove home, Irving said, "Harry is the first-born son. He's the boss. I need my job. Please don't ever criticize, or talk fresh to him again."

137

What? Irving said he and his brothers were partners. Better not tell him that Harry doesn't ring up every sales. Hmm. I think I'll have to have a serious talk with Annie this Sunday.

CHAPTER 50

"Betty, I'm going to eat my lunch upstairs with Mrs. Feller, today." There were no objections, and I took up two plates of food. I pushed the bell with my elbow and waited for Annie to come to the door.

She smiled and looked pleased when I told her that I'd like to have my lunch with her. She brewed Sweet Touch Nee tea, and I set the table.

"Annie, you're a clever woman to have started Feller's Department Store."

"Jack mentioned you were working in the store all week."

"I don't expect you to pay me for it. I had some free time to help out your boys. That business is so successful it supports four families. Right?" She smiled, nodded, and took a bite from her sandwich.

"You have three fine sons. You must be very proud of them."

"I am. My favorite is Irving. He's even more handsome than my Sam was, but don't tell anyone I said that." We both laughed.

"Irving thinks Harry is your favorite."

"Why is that?"

"Harry is your first-born son. He's the boss and will own the store one day."

"No. I want all my sons to own the store together after I'm gone."

"Harry told Irving and Jack that they have to listen to him because he's the boss, and they believe him. If anything happens to you, Harry'll claim the store because he's the first-born."

"Harry can want it that way, but that's not what I want. I want my boys should live and continue to work together at my store."

"So, you want them to be equal partners in the store?"

"Yes. That's what I want."

"Have you made out a will stating what you want done with your property?" "What's that?"

139

"You should go to a lawyer and tell him you want your store to be equally divided by your sons. You protect each of your sons by saying you want them to have equal shares of your store in the event you die."

"Ah, I see. Yes. That's what I want. Nobody lives forever. What I say in my will is what should be done when I'm no longer around?"

"Yes. Then there can be no argument over who owns your property. When do you think that you'll make out your will, Annie?"

"Can you do that for me?"

"I'm not a lawyer, but I'll be glad to take you to see one tomorrow."

"I look sick to you?"

"No worse than last week."

"Ha-ha! That's what I like about you. You say it the way it is, and no bull shit." She finished her tea and said, "I'll straighten out my boys today. Tomorrow, you can take me to see a lawyer in the afternoon."

"Annie, your will must be notarized and signed by two witnesses. Do you want Betty to come with us to be another witness?"

"No. Don't tell her what I'm going to do. She'll snoop around here if I'm not at home. Hmm. Come to think of it… maybe she should come with us. Then,

I won't have to worry about what she's doing up here while I'm not around."

"Harry'll becoming up soon. I'll clear the table and take these plates downstairs. Oh, there's one more thing. You want your sons to stay healthy, right?"

"Yeah. So?"

"It would be healthier for them working in the store if it had an air conditioner."

"If you think it will help my sons stay healthy, then they should have one. I'll tell Harry to get one right away. I'm glad my Irving married a smart girl. I'll see you tomorrow."

Jack and Irving went upstairs when I returned with the dishes. I took them to Betty who was standing at the sink. She added them to the ones she was washing.

"Mrs. Feller wants to make out her will tomorrow. I'm taking her. She asked that you come with us. Okay?"

Betty turned from the soapy water open-mouthed. "What did you do? Hypnotize the old lady? I've been urging her to do that for years. Harry thinks because he's the oldest he should get her store. I've been telling Jack that's just a European custom and not the law."

"Will you come with us tomorrow?"

"I wouldn't miss seeing her do it for all the tea in China."

"Do you know a lawyer nearby who can handle it?"

"No."

"Where's your classified phone book? I'll look one up."

While I scanned the phone book we heard a crash from upstairs. We raced to see what had happened. Betty said, "It would be terrible if Annie dropped dead before she made out her will."

Betty flung the door open. We saw Harry standing wide-eyed and frothing at the mouth. *Is he having some kind of a fit?* He'd knocked over his chair, and his face was crimson.

Annie said, sternly, "Harry, it's my property. I'll divide it the way that I want. Tomorrow, I want you should go and get an air-conditioner for the store."

Three-hundred-pound, six-foot Harry advanced towards me shaking his fist. I saw Irving and Jack shrink back. Neither of them attempted to stop Harry, or make a move to try to protect me… *I'll kick him in the balls if he tries to lay a hand on me.*

Harry shouted, "This is your doing! You think it's easy to run that store? You and that lazy bum you married can do it from now on. I quit."

I remained calm as I said, "A sales clerk is easily replaced, Harry. Irving does the buying for the store. And I'll see to it the new clerk rings up all his sales on the cash register."

Harry's threatening demeanor vanished when I said that. He must've realized I'd seen him pocketing cash at the store. He went white, and opened and closed his mouth without saying anything. He turned from me and smiled at his mother. The brothers looked relieved that Harry hadn't beaten me up.

He said, "Ma, you're right. I'll buy an air conditioner tomorrow. Do what you want. It's your store. I'll see you boys tomorrow." He left, slamming the door behind him.

Harry was a foul-mouthed bully who had made it his business to intimidate, beat up, and put down his younger brothers all their lives. Irving and Jack were terrified of their big brother. They'd never have stood up to him. They believed Harry was the boss, and the rightful inheritor of their mother's store. Irving had rescued me from Mama. I felt happy to have rescued him from Harry's domination.

CHAPTER 51

Next day, Annie, Betty, and I met with a lawyer in the Bronx with whom I had made an appointment. The lawyer wisely said a person who didn't benefit from the will should witness it. We all agreed. His secretary, and the bookkeeper signed it.

The lawyer kept the original. We each got a copy. I asked for another copy to be given to Harry. *Whew*…. I was glad there'd been time for Annie to do the right thing by her sons.

I suggested to the ladies that we go to the Broadway Diner in Yonkers for coffee. Annie was delighted to be taken out to eat. She read the large menu and selected a dish of stuffed grape leaves. Betty ordered a slice of the seven-layer chocolate cake from the window, and I had a dish of vanilla ice cream.

During the table conversation, I learned that neither of them had seen Van Cortlandt Mansion; the oldest house in New York, and in the the third largest park in New York City. I suggested we go there on our way home.

***

A docent met us at the door. It was interesting to learn that the thick stone on stone slab walls insulated the house from both cold and heat. In the kitchen, we learned they'd made the pewter dinnerware they used.

Betty laughed when the docent pointed out that the children of the house were locked in their beds at night. "I wish I had known about that when Roger was a little boy. He was always coming into our bed at night."

Annie asked, "Oh, is that the reason you and Jack have only one child?"

I drove them home, their faces wreathed in smiles. Annie said, "That's the most fun I've had in years. Thank you, Maxine."

"I had a good time, too. See you on Sunday." Betty helped Mrs. Feller upstairs.

CHAPTER 52

I'd seen a sign pointing to West 246th Street on Broadway, and decided to follow that route home. It took me through the Fieldston Estates. I admired the large beautiful homes. I recognized the one Kathren Hepburn had used in the comedy film "Bringing Up Baby". The old oak trees were tall and provided lot's of shade from the sun.

As soon as I reached the Henry Hudson Parkway, I realized it was a much simpler way for me to get home. I'd been using the highways to get over to the Fellers. Riverdale was bounded by the Hudson River on the west side and

Broadway on the east. We lived less than ten minutes from Jack and Betty Feller, yet we had a totally different lifestyle.

I parked the car on the service road. Recalling the sealed boxes Annie had given us for a wedding gift, I carried what I thought were empty boxes up the steep slate steps to my Briar Oaks apartment. Then, I placed them on the floor at the rear of my walk-in bedroom closet. At last, I had time to arrange our clothes in an organized fashion.

***

I went to the garage to look it over. A car was parked in Irving's numbered space. I complained at the garage office. No one admitted knowing anything about the unauthorized car, or that Mr. and Mrs. Feller now rented the apartment to which the space belonged. *Enough of this run-around buck passing.*

I drew in a deep breath and said, "If necessary, I'll show you my copy of the lease. Meanwhile, you have keys hung on the board for each of the autos parked in this garage. If my space isn't vacant by the time my husband comes home, I'll take those keys and charge the owner five dollars a day for parking in my space."

I was certain the space would be available before Irving got there. Also, I could use our space when I shopped for groceries, and needn't carry my packages up the steep hill. Walking up that steep hill left me gasping for breath, and carrying bags loaded with groceries wasn't pleasant. *The garage space belongs to me too.*

I decided to park on the service road overnight. I'd do my shopping each day and, when I came home, use our garage space until Irving returns home.

***

Irving looked sullen when he arrived home that evening.

"What's the matter?"

"Harry hollered at me in front of the customers and ridiculed me all day."

"He'd probably like it if you quit. It would mean more money for him."

"You don't understand how hard my brother works in the store to make the business a success. He's never late. He never takes a day off, or a vacation."

"That's his choice." *Why doesn't Harry take a day off? Hmm. No vacation? He takes the money home, and brings it to Ammie on Sunday. That's a lot of temptation lying around the house. He doesn't make nightly deposits at a bank because his mother doesn't trust banks after her bad experience with them. However, the rules have changed for banks. I'd sooner trust a bank than Harry.*

Maybe he doesn't want them to see how much more cash they'd have if he wasn't there to take it home.

CHAPTER 53

Finally, the delivery strike was over. Our furniture would be delivered in two days. I didn't go to work with Irving that day. My phone rang to inform me they'd loaded the elevator and would start the delivery.

I left my apartment door open for the moving men, and waited in the hallway for them by the elevator. That's how I met my glamorous, across-the hall neighbor, Mary Jane Gordon. She was wearing a pink satin robe, and a matching scarf around her head. She was returning from the incinerator room.

We chatted amicably in the hall while the movers arrived and unloaded my furniture. She watched as the parchment-finished, wood, French Louis XV bedroom set, designed and manufactured by the Mittman Furniture Company, was brought into my apartment.

The king-sized bed had a pink-upholstered, wooden headboard, and a matching pink bedspread. A blue-mirrored, six-drawer vanity fit for Marilyn Monroe arrived. *Wow. I thought the first Mrs. Feller knew what she was doing.*

The men set up a pink marble kabuki-style table in front of the beige kidney shaped couch in the living room. The couch was very comfortable looking, and I invited Mary Jane in for a cup of coffee. We sat on the couch.

An enormous teak- L-shaped desk was installed in the living room where it looked great. I' would only need to purchase a dining room set to complete the furnishing of the apartment.

"Maxine, I'm impressed with your taste in furniture," Mary Jane said.

I told her I'd never have purchased such expensive furniture. "These pieces were selected by my predecessor, but I loved her choices."

"My dear child you must never reveal that to anyone else in the building. It's far too much information to give a neighbor in our community."

The delivery men left, and Mary Jane and me continued our conversation. She had worked and traveled for a cosmetic firm. She taught women to use her employer's make-up. She revealed when she became a widow, she'd left her little girl with her mother. Now, she and her daughter were estranged, and she felt terrible about it.

I told her about my childhood and we realized we could fulfill each other's needs for a mother-daughter relationship. Mary Jane sought a younger woman who could benefit from her sage advice, and I wanted the guidance of a wiser, older woman. So, she and I agreed to have coffee together each day from then on.

We shopped together and enjoyed one another's company. She cautioned me not to tell anyone ours was the second marriage for my husband. She taught me how to take a compliment graciously, and how to give one in a friendly manner.

I admired her greatly, and was glad she was my friend. Later, I learned this was her second marriage, and she'd married a much younger man.

CHAPTER 54

When I hadn't become pregnant on our wedding night, Irving insisted that I see a doctor to find out what was wrong with me. I was worried too. I went and learned after many tests there wasn't any reason why I wouldn't conceive. My doctor advised me not to worry about it. So, I didn't... but Irving still did.

In the morning, I noticed he would peek out the door to see if the hall was clear before leaving the apartment to go to the elevator. *Is he ashamed to be seen here? There was a lot about Irving that puzzled me.*

One evening, I asked him why he checked the hall before he left. "All the men in this building dress in nice suits. I can't go to work dressed like that. What would Harry say?"

"What's the matter? Don't you like looking like a shabby slob like your older brother? Most of your customers dress better than him.

I explored the neighborhood to check out the local private schools. I left my resume at Horace Mann, The Fieldston School, and a Yeshiva.

***

When my husband came home he told me Harry was boasting that I was afraid of him, and wouldn't dare return to the store to face him after what I'd done.

"You can tell your brother that I've applied at the schools in this neighborhood. I have neither the time nor inclination to be a sales clerk all my life."

"I'll tell Harry you're looking for a teaching position."

I had an uncomfortable feeling Irving preferred to side with Harry against me, and had no appreciation for what I'd done for him, and Jack. His loyalty to his older brother caused me to wonder about the future of our relationship.

I was offered the opportunity to substitute for a male teacher's class at one of the schools, and was pleased to accept. I was told he was in the hospital. So, I encouraged the children to write him letters in the morning.

When we returned after lunch several children swarmed around my desk and one of them delivered a karate chop to my right arm. I was in pain and ordered them all to be seated. I didn't know which of the them had delivered the blow.

All of them looked quite smug. So, I said to the class, "I fear for my nation with you future citizens running it. You come from the best homes in the city but you don't appreciate the fact that you attend a pretigous school where you are hopefully being trained to become good citizens. I'm ashamed of you, and pity your parents."

***

During dinner Irving said, "I thought I was a good buyer, but Harry was bragging today that he'd paid a lot less than me for the same merchandise."

"Is he trying to compete with you?"

"I don't know, but he did buy it for a lot cheaper price than I paid. I'll take my time tomorrow, and try to save the store more money."

"If you can't do that, Irving, then maybe you should raise some of your store's prices. You charge less than Woolworth did on many items I once sold there when I was a teenage sales worker there."

"Really? We always let Harry decide what to charge."

The business is still surviving despite Harry. He has no merchandising sense. Oh, well, let them do what they want to do. It's their store. Irving doesn't like it if I make business suggestions for him to implement… Hmm… Irving makes a good living. I'm not greedy. It's better to sleep with my husband than a sullen stranger in my bed. I'm not going to interfere there anymore.

CHAPTER 55

"Irving, your mother didn't look so good to me today. How often does she see a doctor?"

"I don't know. Betty takes care of that."

"Maybe you should ask Jack to tell his wife to take her."

"Maybe you should learn not to tell other people what to do."

There it is. Irving does side with Harry and Jack against me.

At least my mother cared about the welfare of her mother. My husband's family is no better than mine.

Irving came home from work smiling, and not dour looking as was usual. I asked, "What's the good news?"

He said with glee, "I found out how come Harry was able to buy cheaper than me."

"How did he do it?"

"The police came and arrested him this morning. He was buying stolen merchandise from a guy who squealed on him to get a lighter sentence."

***

Harry was away from the store for several days, and business was very slow. So, Irving, Jack and Annie were surprised when Jack brought up the brown shopping bag with money to be counted by her while Harry wasn't around to bring it.

Annie saw there was a lot more cash in the bag than usual. Immediately, she realized that Harry had been stealing from her. She said, "Without Harry skimming, my store earns a lot more than I thought it did. I'm very glad that I made out my will."

Jack related this information to Betty and me when he returned home.

Betty said, "See Jack, that's the reason why Harry never takes a vacation."

I said, "Let's make out a vacation schedule for all of us."

Irving said, "No Maxine. If Harry doesn't take a vacation then I won't take one."

Right or wrong Irving sides with Harry. He believes his big brother knows best and is always right. Why?

***

In the privacy of our home I said, "Irving, I work hard and have earned a vacation. If you don't believe that you've earned a vacation, then don't take one. When I get my Christmas vacation, I'm going with my teacher friends to Miami Beach."

The following day, I told Mary Jane what I'd said to my husband. She suggested that I tell him also that when my friends leave to come back home to work, I'd be staying down there until he came to get me.

I was going follow Mary Jane's advice. Irving had no objection to my going to Miami Beach without him. He phoned me each night. I found it far more pleasant to chat with Irving long distance than to be at home to cheer him up after a long day of Harry's insults to him.

My friends and I stayed at a nice hotel on Collins Avenue. As we sunned ourselves on the beach, I stared in disbelief when the first love of my life, Martin Goldberg came walking toward me.

"Hi, Maxine. I thought you were a married woman. Where's your husband?"

"He's working up north. This is Irving's busiest season. What're you doing here?"

"I'm on my honeymoon."

"So, where's your bride?"

"She's up in the room with a fever, and a bad cold. She told me to get some sun, and just leave her alone 'til she feels better."

"That's too bad. How's your mother?"

"She's all right. Y'know, I'm kinda lonely down here. Would you have dinner with me?"

It would serve Irving right if I did, but I said, "No. I'm here with my friends, and you should be with your bride."

Alice, my roommate said, "He's a real cute guy. Why didn't you make a date with him?"

"I'm a married woman."

"I wouldn't have told anyone if you went out with him. I wish he'd asked me out."

"He's married, too."

"Oh, please …we're all down here to have a good time. Don't be such a prude. Miami Beach is supposed to be a 'choice' vacation spot.

I wasn't spending any part of his honeymoon with Martin. It would be foolish of me to start anything that might jeopardize my marriage. It was already rocky enough.

***

It was diverting to go to the races, and shop with my friends. At the end of two weeks my chums packed and left for the airport. I remained behind. The manager offered me a dramatic cut in the room rate if I chose to stay.

When Irving phoned, I asked him what I should do about the room.

"It's a good deal. Take it. I'm going to join you down there."

"Oh, I've missed you, Irving." He must have missed me, too. I was glad for our marriage's sake that he'd decided to "come on down."

CHAPTER 56

Irving arrived looking thin and exhausted from his busy Christmas work schedule. In the morning, I suggested we go to the beach where he could get some sunshine. He needed a good rest.

"I don't want to get a tan. What would Harry think?"

I thought… *you'd come to Miami to get a tan and have a good time with your wife.* It was brave of Irving to break away from Harry's way of thinking how to live his life, and take this vacation.

"Sweetheart, I'm glad you came. What would you like to do?"

"I don't know."

"They have horse racing, and dog racing down here. Would you like to go?

"That sounds exciting. Let's do it."

Irvin g was great at picking winners at the tracks. "Here are all my winnings. What do you think we should do now?"

"Let's go to the Miami Stock Exchange. I've heard they have the most comfortable seats in town, and free coffee and sandwiches."

"We can afford to buy our own food."

"Irving, when I was a kid, I learned about the stock market, but I've never seen one in action. I'm curious."

"If that's what you want, let's go."

***

The seats were very comfortable. We watched the lighted ticker tape display move around the room with its unfamiliar symbols. I overheard snatches of conversation and realized people in this room were investing large sums. Although there were no blinking lights, tables or slot machines paying off like in Las Vegas, this was another kind of gambling place where you could win, or lose money.

***

153

I told Irving that I'd once purchased stock in a company that produced something I liked and figured that others would also want to use it. It had increased in value, and paid a dividend, too.

Irving surprised me when he said, "A few business owners I know advised me to buy some stocks."

"How did they perform?"

"What?"

"Did they go up or down?"

"I don't know. I put them in a shoebox and forgot about them."

"When we get home, Irving, I'll check them out for you."

"Great. If I made any profit then I want to share half of it with Harry."

Why? I don't understand the relationship between Irving and his brother. He seems more interested in proving to his older brother that he's smart than building a nest egg for us. After we have babies will he continue to be this way? Can I get him to change this attitude?

***

Back at our apartment, Irving took a shoebox from the shelf in our closet and handed it to me. Instead of pairs of shoes, it held shares of stocks.

CHAPTER 57

In the morning, I examined the certificates. Ten shares of International Business Machines, five shares of American Telephone and Telegraph, and five of General Electric. I knew these were good stocks, but I didn't know what Irving had paid for them.

I made an appointment with a broker at E. F. Hutton at their Broadway branch office. I was advised that I would need a Power of Attorney to be able to execute my husband's wishes. Irving signed the document enabling me to act for him.

From the dates on the certificates of stock the broker was able to determine the cost, and the current (1956) price. Irving had been well advised. He'd more than doubled his initial investment. Following my husband's instructions, I ordered the broker to sell one half of the shares in the account, and make out a check for that sum to Harry Feller.

**

Then, I opened a joint account for Irving and me and deposited the remaining stocks into it. I planned to use my teaching salary to purchase more stocks for our portfolio.

Several days later, I picked up the check for Harry and drove to the store to give it to Irving. When I entered, Harry greeted me.

"Hello, Maxine. Long time no see."

"Hi, Harry. Where's Irving?"

"He's in the back getting something for a customer."

Irving climbed the ladder from the basement with a box of shirts. I gave him the check. He read the amount and grinned. "It'll give me great pleasure to hand this to my brother."

Harry took the check from my husband and read it. He hugged Irving, and waved in my direction and shouted, "Thank you." I waved back, and left the store.

I'd thought Irving had chosen to do an extravagant thing with this money. It was an expensive pleasure for a few seconds of thanks. I was certain It would accomplish very little in improving Irving's treatment by his brother. However, I voiced no objection to his doing it.

***

Walking back to my parked car, I noticed a crowd of people gathered at the street corner. A tall black man stood on a large wooden box exhorting them to buy only from black merchants. He fell silent as I approached. I crossed the street and he resumed preaching to the crowd.

If I weren't the only white face there, I'd have shouted, "Buy wherever you get the most value for your dollar."

***

Irving was full of enthusiasm when he got home. He wanted to go to bed with me as soon as dinner was over. *Whoopee!*

***

Next morning I reflected, *If giving that check to Harry caused Irving to revert to the sexy man I thought I was marrying, then I'm glad to have helped.*

That evening, Irving came home upset, and with tears in his eyes. *Had a black mob burned out the store?* My voice trembled as I asked, "What's happened?"

"Harry is claiming that he was cheated. The check should've been larger." "What? I did exactly what you told me to do. Millie and Harry are "goniffs". They're conniving cheaters and believe everyone else is a cheat too. Your brother was very happy with his check. Don't worry. I'll take care of everything."

He sobbed, "Good. See to it that you correct this right away!"

My husband sounds as if he's accusing me of not doing just as he asked. There're none so blind as those who will not see. Right or wrong, my husband thinks Harry's always right. I'm getting fed up with Irving and his family's nonsense.

***

Next day, I carefully prepared for a showdown with Harry. My plan was to arrive a little after closing time. I'd ask Harry to empty his pockets on the counter. This would prove to my husband that Harry was a thief; taking

156

money from the store sales and stuffing it into his pockets instead of ringing it up on the cash register. Then, I'd show Harry the documents in my purse that said he'd received a check for exactly one-half the amount for which the stocks were sold.

I parked the car and sat in it until I saw Jack and the other clerks leave the store. I went to the store door and rapped on it. Irving opened it. He looked very tired. I went in and approached Harry. I said, "I see you have today's proceeds in the brown bag to give to your mother."

"Yeah. That's right."

"Harry, if you'll empty your pockets on the counter, then I'll open my purse and prove to you the check Irving gave you is half the amount of the stocks he sold."

Will Harry show Irving there's store cash in his pockets?

"Ha, Ha," Harry chuckled. "Irving, I've only been teasing you, little brother. You know I trust you. We're brothers." He hugged my husband, and patted him on the ass. "You do a great job, Irving. We need you here. I love you.

Don't take what I say so seriously."

Irving's face relaxed and became wreathed in smiles. He hugged his big brother. So, Harry had managed to avoid emptying his pockets on the counter showing Irving that he was thief. There was no need to open my purse.

***

After that, I was hurt because I'd received no apology from either of them, and further resented *my husband siding with Harry against me. Irving was acting as if he'd found me unreliable. As the days passed my anger and resentment grew.*

CHAPTER 58

The phone rang around seven AM. Irving answered it. His mother had died in her sleep. He was devastated.

We drove to the Feller house. Jack met us at the door. Harry and Millie were finishing breakfast.

Jack said, "The doctor just left. Mom had a heart attack during the night."

We went upstairs to say goodbye to Annie. She lay on her bed fully dressed. I assumed Betty and Millie had dressed her. Two men arrived from the funeral home to take Annie away.

Betty asked me to remain behind and change the bed linens. I agreed and started the task. In the bed mirror, I noticed Betty drop a towel over Annie's jewelry box on the dresser, then she covertly carried it away and went downstairs, After that, I decided I would turn the mattress over by myself.

I pulled back the mattress, and was surprised to see little packages littered the bed. Was this a kind of improvised board for a bad back? Curious, I opened one of the packages. It was full of money!

I wondered, if *Betty would keep everything in the box she'd secreted for herself, or would she share the contents into equal parts? So far, Irving was the only one in his family willing to share, and I was resentful that I'd done it for him yet he'd sided with his brother. Neither one had apologized for doubting my honesty.*

Hmm. Annie didn't want Bettty snooping around. I surmised it was because of her hidden money. I remembered Kim's advice in Lindenhurst, "When in Rome do as the Romans."

I pulled off the mumu dress I'd put over my head this morning when we'd hurried to come over. Then, I lay down and stuffed the packettes into my underwear, and bra. After that, I made the bed. I pulled back on my loose dress, and walked downstairs.

I didn't let on I'd seen Betty sneak away the jewelry box while I was stripping the bed. I decided to wait and see if they would tell me anything about sharing a part of whatever had been in that box. If they did, then I'd tell them about what I'd found.

***

When I entered Bettty's place, the two women were wreathed in smiles. Bettty handed me lots of food to eat. Mollie was friendly, and there was no bickering between them today. No mention was made of sharing any jewelry.

I did notice Betty was wearing a marquis shaped onyx ring with two diamonds, and Millie sported a similar one with three stones. I was shocked. Annie's body wasn't cold, and they were already wearing her jewelry.

Obviously, they had already divided their loot. Only I knew what I'd found. No one else was aware of its existence.

The sandwiches were good, and the chocolates were delicious. I decided not to mention my find. After the food was eaten, Irving and me went home.

During our drive home, a radio newscaster described incidents of hostility continuing to rise in Harlem against white store owners. I recalled seeing one of those street-corner rabble-rousers in action, and I knew most of the store's customers were black.

If something were to happen to the store, then we wouldn't have Irving's income. *Hmm. How could we afford to continue to live in Riverdale?* Annie had intended the money packettes for me. She knew I'd take care of her favorite son, Irving.

I'd been investing all the money I earned from teaching in the stock market, and it was performing well. Annie wanted me to look after Irving. I'd hoped the stock market would enable me to do so if anything happened to the store.

Now, I had more money to invest to make caring for him a reality, if he lost the store.

CHAPTER 59

In the months that followed racial tension kept building up in Harlem. However, business at the store went on as usual. The brothers continued to meet at Jack's place to count and divide whatever money Harry brought with him. Irving kept the store's books for the accountant. Harry paid the taxes.

***

I was on pins and needles worrying. Each night, I was relieved when Irving came home safe, but verbally abused by his brother. The unrest in Harlem continued to grow.

One day, the landlord came to the store and asked Harry if he wanted to buy his building. This proposal was discussed on Sunday at Betty's apartment.

Harry said, "He's asking too much for it. The building is very old and needs a lot of repairs. We'll become the landlords, and have to put up with his tenant's complaints to fix things up."

It was difficult, but I bit my lip, and didn't say a word. I felt it would be better for my marriage not to interfere in any way with whatever Harry wanted to do in the store. Irving wasn't happy working alongside his brother, but I already knew he would side with Harry. It was better for me to keep quiet, and be a supportive wife.

It was 1957, and I believed the store was in a great location. Harry was just short sighted, and stupid not to see it. If it weren't for the uncertainty of racial tension, I'd have used a "dummy" and bought the building; and then doubled the store's rent.

It was a worthwhile investment to go along with our stocks. They were all doing well and earning dividends too. The market was proving to be a good security net for us in the event we should ever need one.

***

Several weeks later a nearby street water main burst. The store's basement was flooded. I learned this wasn't the first time it had happened. However, this time they had flood insurance. Hurrah for Harry.

Cleaning up was wet, nasty work. Irving got sick. He was doing most of the clean-up. He feared Harry would accuse him of being a slacker, and refused my pleas to go to a doctor.

Two weeks later, Irving had a high fever, and was hospitalized. I visited him every day until dizzy spells caused me to consult a doctor for myself.

The doctor examined me, ordered some tests, and assured me I wasn't sick. I was pregnant. Thrilled by the good news, I hurried to tell Irving.

He said, "Harry will respect me when I have a son." *Who cares what Harry thinks about it?*

On Sunday, I went to Betty's house as usual, but I wasn't given Irving's share of the money. Harry said, "If your husband doesn't work then he won't be getting any pay."

I pointed out to him according to the Will my husband was a partner in the store, and not a paid employee. Then, Harry thought it over and said he'd pay Irving's hospital bill. I was upset by this unfair treatment. I related what had happened to Irving. He said, "Never ask my family for anything."

It occurred to me, that *if Irving should die… then my child and I would be without his income. I decided I'd get a lawyer to do my asking. However,* Irving recovered a few weeks later, and went back to work.

***

Severe morning sickness caused me to give up my substitute teaching job at Horace Mann.

CHAPTER 60

Looking around our one-bedroom apartment, I decided I would need to create some space for our baby. We couldn't yet afford a two-bedroom apartment at Briar Oaks.

The dining room was rarely used. With the help of Mary Jane, we pushed the table up against the window. Now there was room for a crib, a changing table, and a place for the baby's clothes. I enjoyed sitting at this table with Mary Jane at teatime and chatting. We'd watch the spectacular sunsets over the river.

The sun would drop from the blue sky into the pink pillows of clouds on the horizon of the nearly black looking river.

The lovely forest below us would darken into a variety of blue blurs as night crept over them. Then, as the sun sank into the river on the horizon, streaks of pink and gold in the sky would slowly dissolve into a velvety blue blanket to end the daylight

Irving would arrive home just as the stars began to appear. I was delighted and felt proud to be pregnant. I looked forward to being called "Mama" by my child. The baby was due in September. I wanted to share my good news with almost everyone I knew in the world.

Mary Jane made me a baby shower, and we invited the neighbors. I regarded her as the mother I'd always dreamed of having, but hadn't known until now. My neighbors were friends with babies and small children.

From our intimate conversations, I knew Mary Jane thought of me as the daughter she'd missed bringing up because she'd had to travel for her work, and I enjoyed our close friendship.

One day, she received a telegram calling her back to her family-home. Her mother was ill. I missed Mary Jane dreadfully while she was away. I was very lonely. I decided to phone my mother. Absence had made my heart grow fonder of her, and my mind forget what she was like.

She said, "Well, it's about time you called your mother."

"I have some good news to share with you, Mama. Can you meet me in Manhattan for lunch?"

"Why should I take a train when you drive a car? You come and get me, young lady."

Since she'd refused to meet me half way, I reluctantly agreed to drive to Brooklyn. I forgot it would take more than two hours to get there and back.

The old neighborhood was an enormous contrast to where I now lived. Mary Jane had taught me how to "fit in" comfortably. I'd learned social graces and mores in Riverdale. *Rich or poor, I preferred to be rich.*

***

It was raining hard when I arrived at 23 Rockaway Parkway. Mama wasn't ready, and went into the bedroom to finish up dressing. I removed my dripping raincoat and left it over a chair in the kitchen. I sat on the living room couch and waited for her. A train rattled past the window on its way to the station.

I remembered how lonely I'd been in this room. Back then, I wasn't permitted to sit on the living room furniture. Although I was now a married woman, I could still feel that ache of loneliness inside me.

Irving expected me to cheer him up each night after Harry had deflated him during the day. I found this futility more and more a drain on my energy. He behaved as if making money was all he needed to do to contribute to his wife's happiness. Maybe it had been enough for his mother, but I was twenty-two years old, and expected more.

Irving rarely touched or kissed me. There was no time for us to go out and have fun. He worked six days a week at the store.

On the seventh he shopped on the east side to refill inventory. I used the money budgeted for travel and entertainment to buy more shares of stock. I hoped my baby would fill the empty space growing in my heart.

***

Mama came out of the bedroom wearing a new floral dress. She posed at the doorway waiting to be admired. It was then that she looked over at me, and noticed I was very pregnant.

She shrieked, "What have you done? I'm too young to be a grandma!"

I was crushed by her reaction, and burst into tears.

She chided, "Don't cry, you'll mess up my mohair couch."

I lept from my seat. "Mother, I'm leaving. I'm sorry that I came. I thought you'd be glad for me. Goodbye." Then, I hurried to the kitchen and pulled on my raincoat.

She followed and said, "Don't be mad at me. You should've told me when you got pregnant. It was a shock to see you with that big belly."

I calmed down realizing Mama was just being her selfish self. *Receiving TLC from her because I'm pregnant was just another fairy tale; like having a caring family with brothers and sisters. Life is tough going, and it won't be getting any easier.* My friend Kate was right, "Life's a bitch, and then you die."

Hold on, Maxine… Mary Jane says to accept people for who they are. Didn't you disappoint yourself with unreal expectations from your mama.

Then, I said, "You look pretty, Mama. Get your coat. I promised you a lunch."

***

My back ached after driving so many hours. I took her to the nearest restaurant. I was uncomfortable in her company. *Why had her attention once been important to me?*

"After we eat, drive me to your home. I want to see where you live. I'll take the train back to Brooklyn."

I thought it to be a good idea. It would lessen my driving time, and I could avoid rush hour traffic after three o'clock.

CHAPTER 61

The idea of showing off to my mother where I lived, and not having to drive her home appealed to me. I was certain she'd brag about my place to all our relatives. I wanted them to know I had succeeded in pulling myself up to a better way of life.

It was my revenge. It never occurred to me Mama would try to use every trick she could think of to move in with us. Mama was delighted with my Riverdale apartment. She insisted on giving me a back rub.

Ah. It did feel good to be pampered. Then, she set to work scouring my bathroom and kitchen. "You need me to do your housework."

Irving arrived with his usual dour expression. He scowled to see Mama in our apartment and asked, "What's she doing here?"

"My mother wanted to see our apartment. She said she will take the train back to Brooklyn."

"Well, she's seen it. Tell her to leave" he said, and headed to the bathroom to take a shower.

"Mama, it's getting late, and the trains run slower later on. This is a good time for you to leave."

"After doing your housework, I'm tired. I'll take a short nap before I go."

Then, she stretched out on the couch. *She probably was tired.* I was at a loss for what to say or do next.

Mama was snoring when Irving came out of the bathroom. He roused her and said, "I'm going to get dressed now, Yetta. Then, I'll drive you to the train station."

"Irving, it's already so late. Can't I sleep here on the couch, and leave in the morning?"

"Absolutely not" and he went into the bedroom to dress. *I had a suspicion that in the morning Mama would probably think up another reason not to leave.*

She turned to me and wept, "I have such a bad headache. Can't I stay here tonight?"

"I'll get you an aspirin."

She scolded, "One day you'll be sorry. Your children will see the poor way you treat your mother, and that's how they'll treat you!"

I realized that showing off was wrong of me. I shouldn't have brought Mama to Riverdale. However, it was good to see Irving was capable of being firm in the face of fire if it didn't involve Harry. It revived my hope he was a capable man. I felt proud of him once more.

"Thanks for your help, Mama. I hope you enjoyed your lunch. Bye. You'll have to excuse me, I need to take my pills now."

"Pills? I'm not leaving my daughter when she's sick."

"Ma, I'm not sick. I'm pregnant. Goodnight."

Irving grasped her by the arm and pulled her out of the apartment to the elevator. I heard Mama shouting, "This is no way for you to treat your mother-in-law" as they waited for the elevator to arrive.

Daddy had advised me to make a good bed for myself in life, but he'd neglected to warn me others would try to jump into it with me.

CHAPTER 62

The contractions were ten minutes apart by the time Irving had driven us to the hospital on Madison Avenue in Manhattan. I was able to walk into the lobby, but stood still gasping in pain. I was ready to deliver.

Dr. Dessauer shouted at me, "Wait until we get upstairs." He helped me into a wheelchair. In the elevator my water broke. The nurse took me to my room to prep me. My doctor left to scrub.

As I was wheeled to the delivery room, I saw a stunning pregnant oriental woman coming from the elevator. I recalled reading in this morning's newspaper about an account of two babies accidentally switched at birth in Great Britain. *That can't happen here tonight I thought to myself.*

***

The doctor thanked me for waiting 'til we got to the delivery room. There was pain as I pushed out the baby. He told me I had a daughter, and had done well. Then, he told someone "Put her out. She did a good job, and needs to sleep."

In the morning they brought a pink bundle to my bed. I unwrapped my baby and stared at the yellow skinned infant. I checked to see if our identity wristbands matched. No one had told me that my baby had prenatal jaundice, and I was skeptical that she was mine.

Mama had often told me the story about my birth. I was pink skinned with yellow curls, and pink fingernails. I was very disappointed with my yellow baby and her straight black hair. *She must take after Irving's side of the family.*

I counted her fingers and toes, and then nursed her. Irving arrived as she finished. "Let me see my son."

"We have a little girl, Irving."

He murmured, "Oh … Well, that's all right. We'll name her after my mother."

"If it is it all right with you let's call her Adrienne, and not Annie."

167

"Yes. I like that name. It sounds very classy."

"I think so too." It was the name on a storefront window sign. I'd seen it from the hospital window across the street on Madison Avenue.

***

A few days later, Irving drove us home. Joe was on duty in the lobby. He remarked on our beautiful "Mandarin princess" and wished us good luck.

One of the neighbors had decorated our hall door with balloons and a congratulation sign. I suspected it was Mary Jane.

I thought, my *dear neighbors are my community; a new family. Real families are accidents of birth, but friends make up a family of choice.*

CHAPTER 63

A year and a half later, I learned I was pregnant again. I waited for Irving to come home so I could share the good news. He arrived on time but looking very worried, and tired.

"Did Harry give you a hard time today?"

"No, he didn't."

"So, what's wrong?"

"The store's landlord sold the building." He sobbed… "We have thirty days to get out. Harry called in an auctioneer, and Jack put the "Going Out of Business" signs on the windows."

"Don't worry, Honey. It's going to be all right. You're a good buyer, and a clever businessman."

"You don't know what you're talking about. I'm nothing without the store, and Harry. I didn't finish high school. Who will give me a job?"

"Over the years you've made lots of business contacts. They know you're a good businessman, and you know how to move their merchandise."

Irving slumped on the couch with his head in his hands and wept. *My husband needs cheering up. This is not the time to tell him about the new baby.*

"Sweetheart, while I've been home, I made it my business to read every book in the public library about finance, and investing. I've learned to diversify our portfolio, and I've invested in the stock market. We have enough money to live on for a few months. I'm sure that by that time you'll find another job. We'll do okay. You'll see."

I was relieved he didn't ask which stocks I'd invested in, or how much money there was in our account.

"You're a good woman. I'm glad I married you. If you have faith in me, maybe things will turn out all right for us. I love you."

"Change is a part of life," I said. "Nothing stays the same. I know you'll play the cards dealt you, and you'll win." *If my husband believes he's a loser he won't see his opportunities.*

It snowed heavily over the next few days, and I didn't take Adrienne outside. I caught up on the housework and laundry. I decided to re-organize the closets.

In the rear of the bedroom closet I found the boxes Annie had given to us long ago. It was time that I opened them… Holy mackerel!

They were full of money. I counted out one thousand, and five-hundred dollars in each box.

It was 1969, and the stock market had fallen considerably. I would've invested this cash in the market if I'd opened them earlier. *Hmm. Irving might've wanted to share it with his brothers. To blazes with that idea. Annie wanted us to have this cash as a gift and we really need it now.*

It assures me we can pay our bills for a long time. Whew…I was uncertain if Irving could find work easily. I feel less worried now.

***

For the next several weeks, my positive attitude buoyed Irving's self-confidence. One day, he said, "~~Maxine,~~ there's a large manufacturer of lady's panties I'd like to be a salesman for, but they don't think they need another salesman."

"Honey, there must be an angle you're not seeing. What can you do for them that their other salesmen can't?"

"Well, their men sell to large department stores. I was a small retailer. Also, I did a good business selling underwear to other retailers. If I can convince them I could sell to a lot of new small business accounts…then they might be interested in hiring me."

"Sounds like a real good idea to me. Tomorrow, go and sell it to the owner, but first go and get a haircut."

In the morning, I laid out my husband's best blue suit along with a fresh white shirt and striped tie. While Irving showered and shaved, I shined his black shoes until they shone. *One must dress for success.*

Irving kissed me and left humming the song, "Bye-Bye, Blackbird." I remembered they'd played it the first New Year's Eve we'd shared at the Waldorf Astoria. I prayed he'd be able to sell his idea.

***

That evening, Irving came home with a sample case, and a bouquet of red roses. I exclaimed, "You got the job. I'm so proud of you."

"Well, I haven't gotten the job yet. The owner, Burt likes my idea, and sees a lot of possibilities in my suggestion. This will be my trial week. At the end of it he'll say whether I'm in, or I'm out."

"I like your haircut, Irving. Don't worry, he's going to hire you." *That night, I was the worried one who had difficulty in falling asleep.*

***

Irving became a million-dollar salesman for Burt in several months. Now he was walking erect with pride. He no longer waited for the hall to be empty before he left for work, and he never again arrived home with a pained expression on his face.

Irving was now the man I thought I'd married. It made me happy he was happy. I was very proud of him, and hopeful for our future.

CHAPTER 64

O n June twelfth our son was born. Irving was surprised he wasn't another girl. He was ecstatic, "I'm better than Harry. I've made one of each." *Men are such children.*

***

Several months later, as I wheeled the baby carriage to the backyard sitting area, Joe, the doorman, praised my husband. He said, "Mr. Feller is such a kind and friendly man. He brings home your new red-haired neighbor every day. Is something wrong with her car? I can recommend a good mechanic."

Hmm. Who was this redheaded person? "I haven't met her yet," and Irving has never mentioned her to me. I wonder if she work near him? "I'll ask him, Joe." After I took a seat in the playground area, I questioned one of the other "bench professors" about the new red-haired neighbor on my floor.

One of the lady's said, "She's a sexy looking divorcee who wears very short skirts." Then, I was told. "Her maid told my maid, "Mistress likes to entice married men to visit her." That woman's a man-eater."

***

I related all this to Mary Jane my savvy neighbor across the hall. "Should I be concerned?"

"You have to stop this immediately, but you need to be very sweet and clever about it."

"What should I do?"

And she told me…

Mary Jane took care of Adrienne while I went to the beauty shop. When I returned, she lent me one of her low-cut, sophisticated dresses, and helped me apply more make up than usual. After that, she volunteered to babysit if I'd continue to follow her advice and meet my husband at the driveway entrance to the garage. And she told me what to say.

***

Dressed to the nines I hurried to intercept him. It wasn't long before his car came to the driveway. I waved to him, and he rolled down his window. The red-haired woman was in the passenger's seat.

"What's up?" he asked.

"I have a sitter. Let's all go to Stella d'Oro for their reopening dinner tonight."

The redhead said, "No thank you," and she slunk out of the car, and hurried away. *She had nice legs.*

Irving said, "I'm glad they've reopened. It's my favorite restaurant around here. I love their Tiramisu. But why did you invite that woman to join us?"

"Oh, I thought she was your friend, and you liked her."

"What? That scatterbrain. She works in the building next to mine. When she forgets her car keys I give her a lift home."

"Oh," I said as I settled into the front seat beside my husband, and I noticed his eyes were glued to the low-cut neckline of my dress.

"I've never seen that dress before. I like it. You should wear more dresses like that one."

At the restaurant, I suggested we get a bottle of champagne.

"It's not a birthday, or anniversary. What're we celebrating tonight?"

"I have an important announcement."

He ordered the champagne and asked, "What's special about tonight?"

The waiter popped the cork, and poured for us. "I want us to toast a new blessed event."

"What's that?'

"Our third child."

"Oh, that's wonderful. When?"

"Sometime in May."

"Great. I couldn't be happier. And I'm glad I have this new job. We can easily afford a third child, but I don't think we should have any more, Maxine."

"Why?"

"Maxine, when we met I didn't tell you the truth about my age. I was scared of losing you. I just knew you were the right girl for me."

I smiled and sipped my champagne. "So, how old are you?"

Irving said that he wasn't ten years older than me. I asked, "How much older are you, Irving?"

"Well, I thought you would think I was too old for you, if I admitted I was seventeen years older than you. Do you mind that I lied?"

The way you've behaved throughout our marriage I thought you were going to say that you were twenty-five years older. What possible good can come of my saying that to him now?

"Irving, you look great for your age." *What am I supposed to say, or do about it now? Can I use this information to my advantage?*

"I look forward to you retiring earlier than you said you would."

"Maxine, I really enjoy my work now, and the way we live. I'm not ready to give it up, or even think about retiring."

When he said that the smile disappeared from my face. My girl friends had thought three years difference was plenty, and to drop him because it was seven years he'd said. Now, Irving is finally revealing he's seventeen years older than me.

I 'd been deceived by him. He'd deliberately lied to me. He didn't consider what was best for me…only himself. He was nearer to my mother's age.

I could very well become a widow with three young children to bring up alone. I agreed we should have no more children. I was scared, and wondered how would I support our children?

He promised he wouldn't die before they finished school. Another lie?

CHAPTER 65

To be a successful retailer, Irving had to sell six days a week. On the seventh, he shopped for the store. With his new job, it was great to have a husband who worked only five days a week. He had time to get to know our children, and more energy to spend with me in bed.

***

We were invited to all the parties of his new employer who was a Sephardic Jew. *Mary Jane said, "It means either you'll be treated as a prince, or a pauper."* Irving was afraid to refuse any of his invitations.

As a result, we were continually being asked to the Bar Mitzvahs, and weddings of his employer's very large family. Also, at least once a month we were summoned for a weekend at the Concord Hotel in the Catskills. This was a lifestyle that neither of us had ever dreamed existed.

Mary Jane pointed out to me this was typical of a "…closed communal society. Social events are used to introduce the youngsters to one another to play, and later to date. Future engagements and marriages are often arranged at these events. Also, business deals are made with friends. They're introductions to trusted friends of friends."

Attending these events, I saw that she was correct. Available women, and teenage girls were decked out in gorgeous expensive clothes. They spoke a language with which I was totally unfamiliar.

Sitting at a table with these strange women who spoke a foreign language while my husband hobnobbed with their husbands was of no interest to me. Rarely did anyone respond if I attempted to start a conversation. All I did was sit quietly, eat, and drink, and be ignored.

***

One night, on another such occasion, I'd had one too many drinks. I was bored, but courageous enough to get up and join in the circle dances. It wasn't that much different from other circle dances. And similar to movements from my exercise classes.

I gyrated along with some of the more attractive belly dancers. Suddenly, I was an instant sensation. No longer was I considered Irving's dud of a wife to be tolerated.

The result of my joining in the fun made Irwin even more business contacts, and the women at the table deigned to speak to me in English. Afterward, we were invited to many more parties, and weekends away from home.

These weekends always included food, card playing, and a hired belly dancing group performing 24 hours a day… *Oy vey. (Oh, dear me)*

At first this was all exciting and fun for me, but eventually the novelty wore off. I missed my children, and my weight started to creep up and up. It worried me. I didn't want to become fat again.

Irving had a hearty appetite yet remained slim. *How did he do it? Another secret he hadn't told me?* I felt angry and was jealous that he could eat and eat, yet not gain any weight. *Life's not fair.…*I was reluctant to accept the next invitation.

Irving became very angry with me. "You should be more supportive of me! I thought you'd be glad for my success. You're thinking only of yourself. Don't be so selfish." Look who is saying that to me?

I complained to Mary Jane. "What am I to do? I don't want Irving to be angry with me, and I don't want to get any fatter."

"Perhaps you should go to my 'diet doctor' and get amphetamine shots to help you keep your weight down. That's what I do when I gain more than eight pounds."

So, hoping to eat my cake, and not wear it around my middle, I went to Brooklyn, and joined a very long line of mostly women waiting to see the diet doctor on Ocean Avenue in Brooklyn.

I recognized a few minor celebrities and comediennes when I finally reached the waiting room. *Hmm. So this is how the rich and famous eat, and still keep their figures trim. Whoopee.*

A nurse weighed me, and told me to sit in the room to wait for Dr. Moses. He came in, and didn't ask me anything about my health. "Roll up your sleeve," he said. He gave me a shot of a colorless liquid. Then, he handed me a box of white capsules and said, "Take one capsule before eating your regular meals. Drink a lot of water. Come back to see me in two weeks."

***

I followed his directions, but had great difficulty falling asleep at night. So, I took a sleeping pill at 2:00 am. In the morning, I awoke with more energy than I'd ever felt before. By the end of the first week I'd lost three pounds. This was wonderful… Effortlessly, I changed all the sheets and did the family laundry; washing and folding, and putting it all away while the children napped.

Then, I'd walk the children to the park, and chat incessantly with the other mothers. When we returned home, I scrubbed the floors while my children napped. I bathed and fed them, and put them to bed.

Not once during the day had I experienced a hunger pang, and I didn't feel the least bit tired, or hungry. This was great!

***

Irving came home with another invitation. When I made no objection to going he was elated. "I'm so glad you understand how important these parties are to my business success."

Then, he hung up his jacket and said, "Hold on to this new cleaning woman. The apartment looks spotless. I hope you'll be able to relax more now. You've been acting very nervous lately. It isn't a good idea to rely on sleeping pills."

"The pills I take to lose weight seem to keep me awake at night."

"Your figure looks great now, Sweetheart. You can quit going to that diet doctor."

"Well, if I start to gain back weight, then I'll need to see him again. Nothing else seems to work for me."

"My boss's wife looks much thinner, but she's not jittery. I'll ask Burt how she did it. By the way, you'll never guess what happened at the office today."

"What?"

"Harry phoned me, and asked if I would get him a job where I work."

"Are you going to do it?"

"Are you nuts? All my life that creep took advantage of me. When I was little, he raped me repeatedly. He always put me down in front of the

177

customers. I want nothing to do with that rat. He'd probably bad mouth me where I work. I wouldn't lift a finger to help him. Let the bum make his own way."

Oh, my poor Irving. How awful it must've been for him. But he was able to change his life. I was glad he'd grown up this past year. Now, he no longer denied the reality of his relationship with Harry. Bravo for Irving.

***

There was no need to be worried about Harry's going hungry. I was certain he'd stolen more than enough money to live on for the rest of his life. What I did suspect however was that Harry really wanted to get away from Mollie's sharp tongue. *What goes around comes around. Serves him right. He made his own bed,*

CHAPTER 66

Getting off the elevator with my children, I saw a young woman sitting on the hall- rug in front of Mary Jane's apartment door. As I approached her, I said, "Hello. Can I help you?"

"I'm Patricia Gordon. My mother invited me here to lunch today, but she isn't at home."

That's not like Mary Jane. "Perhaps she was delayed, or had a flat tire. Please come into my apartment to wait for her. I'm her friend, Maxine Feller."

I offered her some fruit, and a cup of tea, and then fed my children. After I'd put them down for their nap, I suggested to her she ring Mary Jane's doorbell again.

No one had answered, and she burst into tears. "My mother has never been there for me all these years while I was growing up. It was foolish to come here.

She's no different now."

"Listen… Your mother told me many times how much she loves you. She regretted that she needed to work, and wasn't there to spend more time with you when you were young.

There must be a good reason why Mary Jane isn't here to answer her door. I'm going downstairs to ask the Super to use his pass-key to open the door. We need to see if she's at home, and if anything's wrong in there. Please, wait in my apartment, Patricia. I don't want to leave my children alone."

Rudy's wife told me he was eating his lunch when I rang the doorbell. He overheard the explanation of why I'd come to see him. He grabbed his passkeys, and we hurried upstairs.

Rudy unlocked Mary Jane's door. We saw her lying on the living room floor. I hurried to her desk to find her phone book, and call her doctor.

He said, "Get her to the Westchester Hospital emergency room as quickly as possible. I'll meet her there.,"

I yelled out the information to her daughter, and we wrapped Mary Jane in a blanket. Rudy carried her to the elevator.

I couldn't go with them and leave my children alone. So, I gave Patricia my phone number and said, "It's Providence you came here today. Take good care of your mother."

***

A week later, Mary Jane and Patricia moved back to Michigan to live together in the house of Mary Jane's birth. I was sad to see my dear friend leave, but glad she was reunited with her own daughter after all these years.

This was their opportunity to create a new lasting relationship, and I was glad for them.

***

My weight did come off, but the pills had made me nervous, jittery and short-tempered with the children, and my husband. Then, Irving told me he'd learned Burt's wife had gone to a spa in Englewood Cliffs, New Jersey to lose her weight. He decided it was the place I should try next instead of using amphetamines.

It was necessary for me to hire a full- time woman to take care of our children, and the apartment. Would *absence makes the heart grow fonder for my family? Will my kids miss me? Would they prefer this experienced new person over me?*

All I knew about being a "good mother" was what I'd read in books on the subject. Just as I'd learned about the stock market.

***

At the spa, I had time to think about Mary Jane and Patricia. I missed being able to visit with Mary Jane daily. However, I was happy for her. She'd bonded with her own daughter. I wondered if a time would ever come when I would bond with my mother.

CHAPTER 67

Today, Irving complained he was frequently short of breath. I made an appointment for him with our family doctor for the following day.

After a few minutes, Dr. Himes discovered Irving had a heart valve problem that would require open-heart surgery. He recommended a surgeon, but Irving was reluctant to have the operation right away. He insisted, "It's not that bad yet."

Several weeks passed. I noticed Irving had developed a gray pallor. I felt he was afraid to have the operation. I would be afraid too. Irving's breathing became more and more labored. I was very worried about him. Something had to be done to convince him to accept the procedure. He needed more than my encouragement, and the hope it would succeed.

I thought the sooner he had the operation the less damage to his heart, and the easier it would be for him to recover. In desperation, I phoned the surgeon's office and explained the situation to his nurse.

She advised me to contact "Mended Hearts." A group of people who had open-heart surgery already, and members of their families.

They meet at Montefiore Hospital, in the north Bronx. Irving agreed to attend one of their meetings. I thought for him to go readily he must be feeling really bad.

Irving spoke with other men and women who'd had similar heart pains and problems before their operation.

These people were dedicated to sharing their experiences, worries, fears and diets. Fortunately, the surgeon who had been recommended to us was by Dr. Himes was known to this group, and was well regarded.

Buoyed by their recommendations, and the fact he had to sit down every fifteen minutes to recover his breath… Irving agreed to the operation.

I drove him to Montefiore the day of the surgery. He told me en route meeting me was the best thing that had ever happened in his life. He never thought he'd be as happy as he was. He apologized for having given me a "hard time," and not being more interactive with our children, and lying to me about his age.

I realized Irving was giving me a "farewell" speech. Obviously, he expected he was going to die during the operation….

At the red light before we got to the hospital, I turned to him and angrily said, "Irving, if you die, I'll never speak to you again!"

He was surprised to hear what I'd said, and broke into peals of laughter. I pulled into the hospital driveway, and we went into the hospital.

His procedure took more than six hours. One of the women from "Mended Hearts" came to sit with me. She made me promise we would join the organization, and attend meetings, and help others to decide to have the operation.

We were expected to share our post-operative experiences with others. *Payback time, if the operation was a success. Readily, I agreed with her. I thought the concept of helping others by sharing our own experience with those we could help was inspired, and I was happy to agree to share our experiences with others.*

***

The apartment was scheduled to be painted while Irving was in the hospital recovering from his operation. I was glad the fumes would be disappointed by the time he came home.

***

I convinced Burt, Irving's boss, I was competent to cover for my husband while he was recovering. I wanted to be sure Irving wouldn't be replaced by another salesman. So, I had to rely on my maid to be responsible for my children, and home.

I left each morning when she arrived, and returned at night. All seemed to be going well so far. On the way home I'd buy a golden book for her to read to the children.

One night I returned home and found Adrienne in tears and the maid threatening to quit. During bath time she'd read… "Three little children went out to sea. One was white, and one was yellow, and one was black."

After that my bright daughter commented "Black like you" and this had insulted her. She considered herself "chocolate." After that, I went into the bedroom with my daughter to talk to her.

"Adrienne, people dislike to hear words about themselves that they don't like. It upsets them. So, we don't say "old man" we say "elderly gentleman. We don't say "fat lady" we say "overweight woman" and we don't say "black" we say "negro". Understand? and she nodded.

I was relieved when she came to work in the morning. However, I didn't know what I'd find when I came home. To my surprise the maid was wreathed in smiles when I returned. She told me in the morning she'd said, "Adrienne where are your black shoes?" Then, the child had replied, "My negro shoes are in my rainboots."

***

The painters did an awful job in my apartment during my absence. They'd used colors I hadn't chosen. I was furious, and complained bitterly to Rudy.

They offered to redo their job. I was forced to accept their offer now, or live with what they'd done and wait two years to have it repainted. *Bastards try to get you when they figure you aren't in a position to complain.*

My problem now was I didn't want Irving recuperating in our apartment until the paint fumes had dissipated. What was I to do? Where else might I place him?

That night, I read in the Riverdale Press newspaper that a new Holiday Inn had opened off a West Side Parkway Exit about a mile past our 246 Street exit. *Hmm. That place is new, and freshly painted and clean. Irving can have his meals served in his room. I'd easily get to see him each day before I came home to be with the children. His welfare, I thought to be of vital importance to all of us.*

***

Mama knew of Irving's operation, and the lousy paint job that had been done in my absence. She phoned me at Irving's office number to offer her home for Irving's recuperation.

"Thanks, Mama, but I'm placing Irving at a new motel that opened near us."

183

"What? You're putting your husband in a motel? I 've never heard of anything so outrageous. Irving needs care. I can give it to him. Bring him here.

I'll look after him."

"Mama, I'll ask Irving what he would like to do, and then get back to you."

Irving told me I was brilliant to have found the motel. He could order whatever he wanted to eat, stroll around the grounds, and walk in the pool for exercise.

Next day I phoned her. "Mama, I spoke to Irving and he'd rather stay at the motel. It has an excellent restaurant, and a pool. We thank you, anyway."

"Who will change his bandages?"

"He has scars, Mama, and doesn't need any bandaging."

"Oh, I see. I didn't know that. So, you don't need me?"

I heard loneliness and sadness in her voice. "Ma, when things are back to normal, I'll come and help you shop for your groceries. Thank you for your nice offer of help."

In the midst of all this, Irving confessed he'd thought it would've been a good "opportunity for his young wife to be rid of her old husband. Now, I believe you love me, and want me to live."

Hmm. I thought, but said nothing to him about how I resented his suspicions and questioned my love. I'd never betrayed him, or lied to him. When we married, I'd pledged always to try my best to be a good wife, and help my husband, and future children.

During our marriage, I'd excused it was his advanced years, or Harry who was responsible for his poor performance as a husband, and father. Now, I realized it wasn't love to marry me without telling me the truth about his age; he was selfish, and inconsiderate.

His anxiety about me not getting pregnant on our wedding night, and insisting I go to doctors unnecessarily, and go through painful procedures to be sure I'd conceived readily had caused me unnecessary anxieties about myself. I wondered if Irving loved me half as much as he loved himself.

***

Several weeks later, I was feeling amorous, and Irving complained he was too tired. Then, he said, "I realize you're younger, Maxine, and if you satisfy your urges discreetly, I won't object to whatever action you need to take."

After he said that, I felt he loved me not at all. All through our marriage I'd endeavored to help him, and make things easier for him. I wondered if I had done it to protect the man I loved, or the man who was the meal ticket for myself, and our children. Had I used him as the father I never had to support me, and give us a better lifestyle?

Was he actually giving me permission to cheat with discretion? I was confused. He knew I detested cheaters. Was he excusing himself from giving me what I was entitled to as a married woman… knowing I'd never want a divorce?

Should I become a cheat and play into his hands, and start to hate myself for satisfying my human desires? What should I do? Mary Jane was no longer here. When she'd left she hadn't even say "goodbye" or leave me her address, or phone number. I didn't know how to reach her, and felt she no longer wanted me in her life.

Walking into the kitchen, I saw half the luscious chocolate cake I'd served after dinner, and decided to have a slice with a glass of milk. It tasted great. Before I knew it the cake was finished. But I did feel much better.

It was silly of me to eat all of the cake that was left. Everyone knew half a cake should be in the refrigerator. Feeling guilty, I went down to my car and drove to the bakery to buy another cake.

Hmm. Only half a cake had been left. So, I ate half of the new cake in order that no one would know what I had done. I didn't realize I was behaving like a crazy person, but I did feel better because I had stuffed my face.

CHAPTER 68

Mother knew how to use people, but she didn't know how to make and keep friends. Because Irving and I decided it would be good for our children to have a grandparent in their lives, a few months later, I phoned my mother.

"The children are eager to see a film at Radio City Music Hall. Would you like to join us?"

She sounded pleased, and agreed to meet us there. I purchased advance tickets to avoid waiting on a long line outside the theater in the cold winter air.

We waited for her in the lobby. She was late, and the show was about to begin. I didn't want the children to miss the film and asked Irving to take them to their seats while I remained in the lobby.

After fifteen minutes, I decided not to punish myself any further with Mama's rude behavior. I showed a photo of her to the head usher and to the ticket clerk. Then, I left her ticket at the box office for whenever she would show up, and I re-joined my family.

It was a delightful film and stage show. I was glad I hadn't missed too much of it

About fifteen minutes before the show ended, an usher showed Mama to her seat.

She was irate and scolded, "Why didn't you wait for me? That's no way to treat your mother."

The people seated around us were annoyed and murmured, "Hush."

Someone said, "Be quiet lady."

I was embarrassed by her behavior, but had no intention of defending myself in the crowded theater, or reprimanding Mama for being late.

After the show ended, I asked her, "Would you like to have dinner with us at Tofffenetis?"

She replied, "Sure."

I'd realized Mama was who she was, and wasn't willing to change. I realized If I were foolish enough to invite her out again, I'd be sure to give her a two hours window in which to be late…That just might work.

***

A year later, her sister, my Aunt Jean died, and Mama moved to Queens. That cut my travel time to visit her in half. I was glad she'd moved closer. Her new apartment was in a building near to Macy's department store.

I kept a list of clothes and items around the house that needed to be replaced. When my list reached five items, I'd call Mama to schedule a visit. I'd take her grocery shopping and always pick up the bill.

After that, we'd return to her apartment and put her things away. Then, I'd leave the children napping on her bed, and hurry to Macy's to buy whatever was needed.

Then, I'd return with a pizza. We'd wake the children, eat, and then go back home.

This was a fine arrangement until Mama decided to wake Adrienne and give her a bath. The poor child slipped in the tub and fell, gashing her chin. I returned to find my bloody child wailing, and Mama confused and wringing her hands saying, "I only wanted to clean her up for you."

I took my bewildered child to Queens General Hospital Emergency room to get her chin stitched. After that, Adrienne didn't want to visit Grandma anymore. So, I would arrange a play date with one of her school chums whenever it was necessary to visit my mother to fill up her cupboard, and refrigerator.

***

Truth be told, I didn't like to visit her either. After I did her shopping, she'd question me trying to look for some excuse to come and live with us. *It was not going to happen.*

I knew Mama was a lonely lady, but I didn't feel sorry for her. It was her attitude and behavior, which she couldn't, or wouldn't change that had gotten her to where she now was in life, isolated and friendless. She'd made her own bed, and no one wanted to share it.

***

Mid-life self-examination time

I'm a survivor. I wrote my story to look at my past life as an adult, and not a child. In order that I would better understand myself. It mystifies me that friends find it hard to understand how I survived the early part of my life.

After I "snitched" on my dad, I'd held myself responsible for damaging my parent's marriage. I felt I was the cause of my parent's divorce, and considered myself a "bad" child. I tried to be a "good girl".

I was scared mama would throw me out too. Where could I go? I became a docile accepting child. I tried to avoid confrontation. I did as I was told to the best of my ability. I hoped being a "good girl" would please my mother, and she would like me again one day.

Looking back on the past, it has finally occurred to me that my father had intentionally relied on his always curious child to ask questions. He relied on me to expose his transgressions. He didn't have the guts to ask my mother for a divorce.

She was a screamer. I opened the door to get him his freedom. Because of me he could marry a wealthy widow. He didn't care about what might happen to me, or my feelings.

Later, I learned my mother was unhappy with her marriage. She'd married on the rebound when her sweetheart married her best friend. She didn't like being married to my dad.

Nevertheless, I was tormented because I felt I was the cause of her unhappiness. I should not have felt guilty about their divorce, but I was a child.

I'd given each of them the opportunity to be free. They should've thanked me!

In retrospect, I remember Mama as a mean-spirited woman, taunting me to continually succeed at academic tasks she hadn't been able to achieve while giving me hope she'd love me more if, and when, I did succeed.

It must've been frustrating for her when I was able to achieve all she asked of me, and went on to do more than she'd ever expected.

Sadly, my achievements only served to drive us farther apart, and never closer. This greatly confused me as a youngster, and I always endeavored to do my best.

Although I appeared to be overfed on the outside, I always felt empty on the inside. "Such a pretty face. It's a pity she's so fat" were words I often heard while growing up.

In my defense I'd say, "I want to be loved for my brain, and not my pretty face." However, I did want to have a boyfriend, and managed to lose weight by throwing up my food. I recall thinking at age sixteen my life would soon end. I couldn't imagine surviving beyond that year.

Isadore, my first boyfriend, stayed with me the evening of my sixteenth birthday until my mother came home from work. I was still frightened, but went to sleep.

Another day dawned, and I was still struggling day by day to survive.

Years later, I learned others have difficult crossroads to overcome too as they age. Forty-five was my next crisis crossroad.

I was uncomfortable, and asked myself…How come this particular birthday is bothering me so much? What have I not accomplished in my life?

Then, I admitted to myself I was jealous of my children. They had a mother and a father. They would get to travel, and see the world.

My husband would not agree to go further than three hours from our Riverdale home, and he insisted we take our children on our vacations. *Life's not fair.*

Life's not fair? Or am I too chicken to ask for what I want? Is my husband indicating he doesn't want to be alone with me?

One of my coworkers at Brownstone Studio, where I now worked, was flying to London, England for her vacation. That sounded to me like an interesting vacation destination.

I discussed going there with Irving. He said, "No."

I told him I was going to buy two tickets to London. "If you don't want to come with me, then I will take our oldest daughter."

Our daughter overheard me and said, "Dad you should go with mother. It will be great fun. I'll take care of my brother and sister while you're gone." I thought her to be a loving and caring teenage daughter.

He said, "Well, maybe I'll go." We three applied for, and each received our passports. I bought two plane tickets. When the date of departure arrived, my daughter said: "I can't believe Daddy has decided to go to Europe with you".

She repeated it over and over again as we carried our bags to the taxi. My daughter had told her friends she was going to London with me, and was very disappointed.

"I'll bring you something nice from London."

***

The "travel bug" bit my husband. Irving told me we should go to Paris the following year. He'd decided he wanted to bed me in every large capitol of Europe. *Whoopee! Our staid marriage was back on track.*

CHAPTER 69

"I'm glad to hear that you're happy." *I've done a good job for him, and he hasn't stopped me from doing whatever it is that I wanted to do.*

Grandma had predicted that I'd end up an old maid living with my mother. Irving had been my chance to avoid that. I suspected that it was partly the reason that I wondered if I truly loved him. Was it enough to commit to a life with him when I agreed to our marriage? I had lived up to all my promises and he had too. I considered that we were both lucky to have had a successful marriage despite the difference in our ages.

"When you're ready to retire Irving, where would you like for us to live?"

"Someplace warm. I guess."

"I've read about the Isle of Rhodes in Greece. It's supposed to be a lover's paradise."

"Oh? Let's go see it next year."

CHAPTER 70

"The cascading gardens of the colorful flowers over the white buildings on the island of Rhodes were indeed a romantic sight. We were glad that we had decided to come here. After a nice lunch of Spanakopita at the hotel we walked hand in hand down a path that led to a park. I sat on a bench beneath a shade tree.

Irving stretched out and put his head on my lap. Then, a well- dressed gentleman approached us and asked, "Excuse me, are you Americans?"

We nodded and then he begged, "Please talk to me! All I ever hear around here is Greek. The harsh sounds of this language hurt my ears. I married a Greek woman to be accepted as one of them, and now I'm stuck living here."

It had been a chance meeting, and a lucky one for us. We were surprised to have heard this fellow's lamentations. We became immediately disenchanted with the idea of living on this beautiful Greek island.

It was better for us to retire in the United States. We considered his retirement more carefully now. Language, food, water, customs, weather, and medical attention were topics we hadn't considered before. *Thank you, G-d for sending that man to us.*

Irving said, "When you find the best place for us to retire, then I'll consider retiring." He suggested we use his vacation time to visit Miami Beach next year. So, I made arrangements for us to go to Florida the following year.

CHAPTER 71

Mama was lonely, and became increasingly demanding of my time. I offered to find her a place in a retirement home, and she became indignant "You have the audacity to suggest such a thing to me.".

Our children had "left the nest", and finding the right place for us to retire to was upper most in m my mind. *It was difficult for me to say "no" to her demands. I needed to move away from my mother. Irving's retirement was a perfect excuse to do it.*

After services at the Riverdale Temple, I spoke to several of my friends about living in Florida. We'd only been to Miami Beach in the months of December and January.

I wasn't pleased to hear the weather wasn't pleasant there all year round. I could expect insects, and mildew issues everywhere. I came to the conclusion every place had some drawbacks.

***

We went to Miami Beach on our next vacation. The day we arrived the sun was shinning, and the air was temperate. I unpacked while Irving sat at the pool and worked on his tan.

The following day it rained, and the weather turned cooler. Guests at the hotel gathered in the lobby to watch television. There was a panel discussion on which state was best for retirement, "Florida or California?"

The Florida physician on the panel said, "As people grow older they need something each day to discuss." He conceded California did have better weather than Florida, but insisted the weather in Florida was unpredictable which made senior living in Florida more desirable than in California.

Irving and I looked at one another and wordlessly agreed we could find something other than the weather to discuss.

"Maxine, find out where in California we should go for our vacation next year."

I phoned my sister, Selma, who was now a realtor in the San Francisco area to ask where in California she thought I should look with the thought of retiring in mind.

"Maxine, I have a listing only a quarter of a mile from my home to show you. You can stay with me while you take a look at it. Why not come out here for a visit, and explore your options.

I informed Irving of our conversation. He said: "Burt's wife just came back from visiting their son at Berkley University. It's in Northern California too.

She said it had rained a lot, and the weather was colder there than in New York City. It doesn't seem like a good place for us, Maxine." *Selma doesn't just want us to live closer. She wants to sell us a house.*

After that, I spoke with my Brandeis club bridge- friends about Irving's possible retirement. I learned about a place in Southern California named La Jolla. "It's Heaven on Earth" my friends all insisted.

I phoned Selma, and told her Irving wanted to live in La Jolla, the southern part of California. She said, "You'll learn the prices of those houses are astronomical, because the weather is so good. It's a beach resort area not unlike Fire Island on Long Island, New York. The parking is very difficult in the summertime. During the winter it's easier to park. However, the storekeepers cater to vacationers, and the prices there are higher for food, and clothes.

The people who own houses there are snooty, and not particularly friendly."

"Well, thanks for the warning, Selma. I thought, we'd take time to explore the surrounding communities when we go there on our next vacation. What

Selma had said was also said about the Riverdale area too."

CHAPTER 72

The weather was perfect every day in La Jolla. The sun shone brightly over the Pacific Ocean. I attempted to go swimming, and was shocked to find out the water was very cold. I'd assumed the Pacific water was warmer than the Atlantic Ocean. Perhaps it was because of all the photos in travelogues showing Polynesian islanders cavorting in the Pacific that gave me that false conclusion.

However, I soon found out it was certainly not true of the Pacific Ocean which met the La Jolla shore. There was a long wooden boardwalk for us to walk along, and benches to sit upon to watch the waves crashing onto the shore.

"This place seems very nice" my husband commented. I agreed. It was an enjoyable stay. I was disappointed to find Selma was accurate in her assessment of La Jolla property values.

On the plane homeward, we took what we thought were our seats. When the stewardess asked the couple seated behind us if they were the Fellers, and had ordered Kosher lunches, I realized we'd taken the wrong seats.

I explained that I'd made a mistake. That's how we met the couple behind us. They knew we were in the wrong seats, and had waited with amusement for us to recognize it. They introduced themselves as Elaine and Bob Weinstein. They lived in a place called Rancho Bernardo in San Diego.

After lunch, the men asked if we minded changing seats so they could play gin rummy. This gave me the opportunity to chat with Elaine. She told me she had heard on the radio Dr. Art Ulene said "Rancho Bernardo was the eleventh healthiest place to live in the world to live."

I was impressed with this information, and told her we were searching for a place to retire. She took my address and promised to mail me the rental listings from her newspaper.

In the course of our conversation, she told me of the tragic death of her son in New York City. It was the reason she and her husband were on this flight.

I was a sympathetic listener. Elaine gave me her address. *If she forgets to contact me then I can write to her…*Elaine didn't forget her offer to help us, and sent me the local newspaper.

However, Irving became very busy when it was time for us to take our usual vacation. He asked me to go to California by myself, and to take along our dog.

I wasn't going to rent a house, live by myself with a dog, and no friends. I had no idea of where to go to eat, or go for entertainment. So, I made arrangements to stay at a hotel near Rancho Bernardo who accepted dogs.

My youngest daughter and her husband took a room at the same hotel to keep me company. However, they had to go back to school a week later. The hotel concierge asked me, "What's the matter Mrs. Feller? You're an "up person" and you look "down."

"Mary, I can't locate a place to rent in Rancho Bernardo that will accept dogs"

"Nonsense. I have a realtor friend in San Diego. Shall I call her to get you a place there?"

"Yes, please do."

The following day she said, "My friend is too busy renting commercial property in downtown San Diego. However, she gave me the telephone number of a good realtor in Rancho Bernardo who will be able to help you to find a place."

"Thank you so much for your help, Mary."

***

The following day, a Caldwell Realtor arrived. He seemed a pleasant enough fellow, and was a good driver. "Over there's Rancho Bernardo" he said as we drove along the highway.

I saw stucco houses and tiled roofs. It made me feel as if I were back in Greece. He left the highway. He didn't drive right into the center of town, and I was puzzled.

He said: "I'm going to show you a place you can rent with your dog, but you'll have to rent furniture too."

He drove to a complex of condos. It reminded me of a place in Arizona when I'd visited my oldest daughter. It was the kind of place which rented to young business people. Therefore, I would be alone at the pool nine to five PM. I didn't like his idea for me.

"I'm sorry, but I'm a people person. This is not where I would want to rent."

"I'm a realtor here in Rancho Bernardo. I know there are no other available apartments to be had here. There might be a room to let, but I don't think an owner would be willing to take you with your dog."

"Please, would you drive me to the Temple where I can leave my name?"

"Sure. I'll even take you over to two senior resident communities to see if anything is available there."

As he drove, he chuckled to hear me praying for help from above. He asked, "Do you ever get a response to your prayers?"

"Often. That's why I continue to pray." He was surprised to find two available rooms listed on the bulletin board.

"Mrs. Feller, I'm going to drive you to my office. You can use my phone to call these numbers. Then, you'll still have time to call and rent furniture for the apartment I showed you earlier." *Is he subtly laughing at me?*

I made the first call, and was refused because of the dog. I prayed again," G-d I need a place to live with my dog." After that, I made the second phone call.

A woman answered. In the background I could hear a dog barking". I mouthed, "Thank you G-d". The woman told me she'd shown the available room to someone earlier in the day who hadn't called back to take it.

I asked her if I could see the room. She didn't object. The amazed realtor drove me to her house. She agreed to rent me the room on the condition that our dogs got along with one another.

My dog never barked and got along with all the dogs in the building where I lived. Her dog barked at anyone who passed by her condo, and got along with no other dogs she warned me.

The next day, she was surprised when our dogs got along well together. She agreed to rent me the bedroom She included the use of her visitor's bathroom.

My realtor was so impressed I'd gotten what I'd prayed for he refused to take the fifty dollars I offered him for his help.

CHAPTER 73

Irving was delighted to hear that I was now living in Rancho Bernardo, and had rented a car. He told me that he wasn't interested in retiring from his job. *He's gotten me out of his hair. I'm not there asking him to retire any more. Had he been manipulating me all along?*

Irving had told me that he'd retire at seventy-two, then seventy-five, and now he was seventy-seven. For several years, I'd been asking him to retire yet he'd never before admitted that he didn't want to quit working.

In truth, I was enjoying living in sunny California away from my irritating mother. I did miss the four seasons of New York City. *Variety in the weather is very nice, but dirt and snow and ice I could easily learn to live without. Would I be content to live in one room and have my husband visit me on holidays?*

Our children had left. Most of my friends had moved elsewhere, and the charm of Riverdale had diminished when new buildings were erected which resulted in the destruction of the forest and now blocked my view of the river.

Irving wasn't interested in our marriage bed. One of the scantily clad models at the showroom had once asked me if there was something was wrong with her because my husband didn't respond to her like all the other men in the office had.

I replied: "He's just true blue."

She said, "Oh, you're so lucky, Mrs. Feller" and I smiled at her.

Now, I looked in the mirror and thought, "Maxine, this is the time for an honest reality check. Irving is a lot older and he's entitled to be happy with what he likes to do. *I was passed expecting more from him. I knew that he would want to work in that office even if he didn't receive a salary. Don't be selfish. Be happy for him.*

I busied myself with visits to my sister and Zack, her husband. However, they were such heavy smokers that I often felt that I couldn't breathe the air in their San Francisco home. Often, the smoke in the house was thicker than the fog outside.

Then, I suggested that we meet in Los Angeles once a month to see a show, or go to the opera.

Ann, my landlady enjoyed it when I left my dog at home. She thought that her dog was in love with Maui because he'd whine at the window whenever she was away.

Several weeks later, I parked my car and saw a "For Sale" sign on Ann's lawn.

"Ann, I didn't know that you wanted to sell your house."

"That sign isn't about me. That's the way the realtors around here try to attract interest in a new listing. They put up a series of signs leading to the house that's for sale."

Since I had to walk Maui, I decided to follow the signs and make it into a treasure hunt to find the house for sale.

It was four blocks away. I saw that it was a Caldwell Realty house listing. So. I called the nice broker who had helped me to get the room with Ann.

Next day, he came and showed me the house for sale, and then he said, "I showed you the house that you wanted to see. Now, I'm going to show you the house that you're going to buy." *That isn't the way to sell me pal.*

Out of courtesy to him, I went with him to see the house that he was talking about. It was on the next street. The house was nicely designed, but the color of it was an ugly brown hue with a pale gray composite roof. He unlocked the door and pushed it open. An orange shag rug and bluish white painted walls confronted me. *Ugh…* I asked, "Are you color blind?"

"Yes. I am. Why did you ask me that?"

He doesn't see what I see. Well, he's a realtor. Let me see if I can see why he recommends this house to me through his eyes. The entrance didn't open to the kitchen. It was not visible and it had a door.

Stain marks on the rug showed me that the former owner had used heavy dark styled Spanish furniture. *The room seemed to scream out to me, "I was meant to be Japanese."*

We walked through the house into the backyard. It was merely a variety of different kinds of cheap grass, and then we walked up the hill to the second tier of the backyard.

When we reached the top, I turned to look at the view, and my breath was taken away. The rocks on the mountains in the distance appeared to me like the crown of G-d. The tightness I'd long felt around my heart suddenly loosened.

I'd never experienced anything like this. *I'd come to the end of a long search.* Whew. It was both pleasant and unsettling. This house might really be meant for me. Could I afford it?

"How much did you say they're asking for this house?"

He gave me a number that I suspected was much too high. I gave him a counter offer that was twenty-five per cent lower than the asking price.

"I'd be embarrassed to give that bid to the Lovelady's."

I had read that it was customary to offer ten percent lower than the original price offer. I was thinking *that the owners don't live here, and nobody wants to pay two mortgages a month.*

"They have the option of turning me down. Meanwhile, I'll consult with my husband, and ask him to come here and see this place. *"I can always raise my offer if need be. Also, it's possible that they might accept my low- ball offer.*

I phoned Irving at nine EST, and asked him to come and see the house I'd found. "Maxine, do what you want to do. You'll do it any way," *he had said this to me one time too often.*

In the past, whenever Irving had said those words in that tone of voice I'd drop the subject, and say and do nothing more about it. This time I decided to assert myself.

Irving had been honest. He declared that he didn't want to retire. I had no control over that. I was living in Rancho Bernardo as neither fish nor fowl, neither single nor married. I felt if I were to continue to live here alone then I deserved to have a nice place to live, and not just a bedroom.

"Maxine, I do have good news. The tax refund we've been waiting for has arrived. What do you want me to do with the check?"

"Please, mail it to me, Irving. Goodnight, dear."

The following day, I phoned Selma. She was real estate savvy, and would agree that I should buy a house of mine own. She asked me to send her photos of the house that I was interested in buying. I did.

A week later, she phoned me and said, "If they're willing to take the price you offered, grab it, Maxine. You can't go wrong at that figure."

I went to the bank, and the manager told me that it was unusual for a married woman to buy a house without her husband. I showed him that I had a Power of Attorney and was using our joint brokerage account as collateral.

Then, he agreed to give me a loan. I needed money for a down payment if the owner was willing to sell.

Less than two months later my realtor phoned me to tell me that I was a very lucky lady. The owners had accepted my offer. They could no longer afford to pay two mortgages a month, and were willing to let the house go.

"I was happy and at the same time worried about owning a house. I'd only lived in an apartment where someone was always available to fix anything that went wrong.

First thing I did was to have the house painted white. Next, I purchased insurance from the agent that my realtor recommended. There was much more that had to be done to the house before I would be able to move in.

I had signed a lease with Ann and continued to live at her house. However, I decided to do the laundry in my own house and no longer needed to use the facilities of the coin operated Laundromat.

I went to the bank and purchased a roll of quarters for my washer and dryer machines. Then, I went to my house to do the laundry. I was baffled not to be able to find a slot to insert the quarters. There was no instruction book for the machines. I decided to ask one of my neighbors how to use the machines.

No one answered the doorbell across the street. So, I walked around the corner and rang the doorbell of The Hoaglin residence. A tall pleasant woman came to the door, and I introduced myself. Then I asked her to show me where to insert the quarters in my laundry machines.

"What is it you want?"

"I have to do my laundry. Please come with me. I live around the corner."

She accompanied me. As we walked, I explained to her that I'd never owned a house before. "For the past forty-five years, I've only used the laundry machines in the basement of the building where I lived, or a local Laundromat."

"It's no wonder that you don't understand. Machines in your home don't require quarters to use them. I'll be glad to show you how they work, she laughed," I thought you were pulling my leg.

My name is Ruth. Ask me anything you want to know about your house."

We shook hands, and after the clothes were in the washing machine, I made us coffee.

CHAPTER 74

O ne day, I did the wash then put it in the dryer. I was hungry and decided to eat lunch while the clothes dried. I drove to a nearby restaurant. Then I returned home to fold the dry clothes.

Unlocking the front door, thick black smoke engulfed and choked me. I ran to Ruth's house to call the Fire Department.

The operator asked, "Where's the fire located?"

"I gave her my address."

"Which room is it in?"

"The fire is in the house, and I am not going back inside to see which room it's in."

In less than five minutes the fire truck arrived. I was relieved to see that the fire hydrant was on my street corner. *This house is in a very good location.*

The Fire Chief told me faulty bearings in the dryer had caused the fire. I didn't understand what he was talking about, but I was glad that the fire was out and that my house hadn't burned down.

Ruth insisted that I come back to her house and call my insurance agent. He arranged for the adjuster to examine the damage.

When the adjuster came, he said, "These walls are a real mess. You have a lot of smoke damage here, Ma'am."

"What does my policy cover?" I asked as I handed him my policy.

"I see the agent sold you a "line of sight" inclusion in your policy. We'll pay for a complete paint job in your home."

What luck! "Does the company have a painter to do the job? Or, do I need to hire someone to paint the house?" *This fire has saved me a lot of money.* I bought a new washer and dryer with part of the money that I received. After the paint fumes had dissipated, I brought a measuring tape to measure all the rooms for a new rug. Kneeling to measure in the hallway leading to my bedroom I felt damp places.

I phoned a plumber to find and fix whatever was wrong. He wasn't sure if it was a leak from the air-conditioner or a broken pipe in the slab somewhere under the floor. He suggested that I get the local water diviner to check out the source.

There is such a person? It sounded like hocus pocus to me yet I phoned one that I found in the phone book.

The man came armed with a "Y" shaped wooden stick, and I watched him, fascinated as he probed and walked with the stick until it dipped to identify the source of the leak. It was under the floor.

I phoned my insurance man to ask if I was covered for water damages and resulting rug damage in my house?

He assured me that I was covered. I breathed a sigh of relief. He offered to come over and see what had to be done. I accepted his offer. *Did I buy a lemon of a house?*

I showed him the damp places that were now visible dark wet spots on the surface of the hall rug. "It's a good thing that I sold you a line-of-sight policy inclusion. You'll need new rugs throughout the house after this repair has been done."

Ah, this is a lucky house for me. The insurance company paid for the paint job, and now they would pay for the new rug. *I'll be able to afford furniture and linens sooner than I'd thought.*

CHAPTER 75

Ann was up and dressed when I returned after walking both dogs. "Maxine, there's a good Estate Sale over in Bernardo Heights this morning. Want to come along with me?"

"What's an estate sale?"

"When people move and don't need all they got they sell it cheap."

There was nothing else that I was planning to do today, and I agreed to go with her. When we arrived at our destination, we saw a line of people in front of us.

However, Ann was a friend of the woman at the door. She motioned Ann to go in ahead of those on line and Ann pulled me in along with her. I felt embarrassed by the glares of women on line.

It was surprising to see such nice couches, lamps, linens, and tables for a fraction of their original cost. I purchased several items and paid to have them delivered to my home the next day. Afterwards, Ann drove us to the shopping mall for ice cream.

After buying so many nice things at such a great price, I wasn't afraid to buy a bed at the mall. One furniture store was going out of business, and I snapped up glass and brass shelves at seventy percent off. *I'm saving more than I'm spending.*

Ann acted annoyed to see that I had money to spend on whatever it was that I wanted. She was okay for a landlady, but not my choice for a friend.

The phone rang as we entered her house and Ann answered it. "It's for you" she said, and handed me the phone.

A lady I'd met at the Clubhouse wanted me to play bridge with her tonight.

She asked me not to bring Ann. I replied, "Sure. No problem!" I wrote down the address.

Ann asked if I was going out tonight, and I replied, "Yes."

"Maxine, where are you going?"

"Out with friends." *She's my landlady, and not my mother. I was glad that my lease was up next week.*

In the morning, Ann claimed that my dog had peed on her couch. How did she know it wasn't her dog? "I'll give you ten dollars to have it cleaned."

She said angrily, "No. I'm entitled to more than that!"

There was no reason for me to stay here any longer. "Ann, my lease is almost up. I'll leave today. Then, you can rent out my room sooner and you'll make up the difference of whatever you think I owe you."

She looked surprised by my calm response. "You don't have to do that, Maxine."

I said nothing more to her, and went to pack my clothes. Then, I carried my bags out to my car. I returned to place Ann's house key on her kitchen table while she was drinking a cup of coffee.

"Would you like a cup of java with me?"

"No thank you, Ann. Goodbye."

I put the leash on my dog, and we left. It was good to have a place of my own to go to, and not put up with any one's nonsense. *I won't take crap from anyone any more.*

CHAPTER 76

At the end of the month, I met Irving at the airport in San Diego. He said, "Hello sweetheart. You're looking great."

I took him to the Lighthouse restaurant for lunch. He admired the ocean view,

"Maxine, you've really learned your way around San Diego. I'm proud of you."

"I took your advice, Irving, and did what I wanted to do. This is the place where I want us to live when you decide that you want to retire."

"Well, I'm glad you like your landlady that much."

"Oh, I'm no longer living with Ann."

"So, where do you live now?"

"After lunch we'll drive out to the house." "House? What house are you talking about?

"The one you told me to do what I wanted with…You'll see it soon."

"Where did you get enough money to buy a house, Maxine?"

"The bank loaned it to me."

"I said for you to do what you wanted, but I never thought you'd be able to get enough cash to buy a house!"

"Irving, it's a done deal. I don't mind that you enjoy your job and now I'm enjoying my retirement. Whenever you're ready to retire you can come and join me."

"I'm angry that you bought a house without me."

"Irving, I asked you to come and see it. You said you were too busy, and that I should do what I wanted to do, and I did it. Why are you angry with me? I only did what you told me to do."

"Well, I should not have said that when I didn't mean it."

"I don't read minds, Irving. Eventually, I know that you'll be glad that I bought it for us."

He grumbled, "How can I ever like it?"

"Well, first you can take a look at it. Are you ready to go?"

Irving sat sullenly beside me as I drove to Rancho Bernardo. "The house still needs a lot of work on the outside, but the landscaper hasn't yet kept any of our appointments. One of these days I'm hoping that he'll show up, and I can tell him what I want him to do.

"Maxine, you're getting a lot of practice telling people how to do what you want done." I glanced at him and realized that he resented that I knew what I wanted.

"Yes Irving, living here without my husband has done that for me. Thank you."

I felt that he was ready not to like the house. So, I pulled up in front of our neighbor's house and asked, "What do you think of this house?"

He glanced at it and said, "I don't like it."

"I suppose that you like the house across the street better?"

"He looked up and said, "As a matter of fact I do. The paint job is better looking than this one. Gravel is far more practical than grass, and less expensive to maintain. See Maxine, you should've waited for me before you bought your house."

Then, I started up the car and drove into my garage. Irving looked surprised, and then he started to laugh.

In the rear-view mirror, I saw the truck of my elusive landscaper pull up in front of the house. Quickly, I got out of the car and hurried to speak with him. As we walked towards the backyard, I explained I wanted to achieve with the garden, and insisted that he put a sewer line in to the street curb.

He said, "Woman! This is San Diego, what do you need a sewer connection for? It's a lot of hard work for me, and it's really not necessary."

"Please, do it."

He smiled and said, "Okay, Lady. I'll start tomorrow?"

It occurred to me that the noise might disturb Irving. I said, "My husband is here. I'd rather not disturb him. Can you start next week?" "Look lady, I'm a busy guy. It's tomorrow, or next month." "Okay, okay. Start tomorrow." This job needs to be done.

I returned to the car, and Irving said, "I've traveled 3,000 miles to be here with you, and you're more interested in your house than you are in me?"

"Sweetheart, I'm sorry, but that guy never showed up when he was supposed to, and I just had to speak with him. It won't happen again."

The following day, digging noises began at 8:00 am. Irving was furious at the noise, and with me. I was angry with the landscaper, and our dog Maui was barking at the workmen.

"Irving, let's go to the race track in Del Mar."

"Let's go anywhere to get away from this noise."

I was grateful that we had won five races, and Irving was in a much better mood.

"How long will it take for your house to be livable, Maxine?"

"'I'm sorry that I wasn't able to get everything completed before you came, Irving, but the landscaper didn't show up for any of our appointments."

"Let's go to La Jolla and stay there for the rest of my vacation."

"They won't allow Maui to be with us in La Jolla."

"Then, you come and visit me"

"What?"

"Is the house more important to you than me? I waited 'til the children were grown and gone for you to be there for me, Maxine. I won't play second fiddle to a house."

What? Maybe, it's my fault that Irving believes he's the most important one in the family. I always had to be the disciplinarian. He was Mr. Nice Guy" and continually undermined my authority. I had to do it all and with no cooperation from him.

"Irving, until now everyone was more important than me in our family."

Nightly, I was the one who bolstered you up after Harry had deflated you. Can he really believe that I ignored him?

"You're over-reacting to this petty inconvenience." *He doesn't see his self-centeredness throughout our marriage. I'm getting fed up with his behavior.*

"You're not going to offer to help me with anything?" *He still expects me to fix things up to accommodate him.* "Irving, I'll drive you to La Jolla if you like, but

I won't join you there."

"Maxine, it sounds to me like you're ready to divorce me."

He's selfish. Irving knows how I feel about divorce, and he's taking advantage of it. Enough is enough.

"Irving, you have to be honest with me. You're not interested in retiring. You have only been sending me away to find us the perfect place to retire in order to keep me from complaining to you about retirement. Well, I'm tired of being neither married nor single. I deserve companionship. Perhaps, divorce is the answer."

"What did you say? You can't really mean that, Maxine."

"I need time to think things over, and so do you."

"Irving, I must drive back to walk the dog. Meanwhile, you can decide if you want to stay in Rancho Bernardo with me, or not. I will drive you to La Jolla if you want, or take you to the airport."

"You've ruined my vacation, Maxine. Take me to the airport. I'm going to divorce you."

I won't beg to stay married to him and be his vacation wife. I'm fed up with things the way they are. Enough is enough.

CHAPTER 77

Several days later, Irving phoned me to ask, "When are you having the papers served?"

"What papers?'

"The divorce papers."

"I haven't had time to see a lawyer yet."

"Maxine, when are you going to do it?"

"It was your idea, Irving. I thought that you were going to do it."

"Oh? I thought that it was your idea."

"Maybe I should come back to Riverdale, then, we can discuss it?"
"That's a good idea. Goodnight, Maxine" and he hung up.

The following morning, the landscaper brought me a bill for the materials he was planning to use. I walked to his parked truck and recognized that brand. It was loaded with inferior cement to be used for my pathways.

I said "Stop unloading these cement bags. Yesterday, I priced all the cements at Home Depot. I won't let you charge me the higher price for the inferior brand of cement. Take it back. I want the higher grade for the price that you're charging me."

Reluctantly, like a kid with his hand caught in the cookie jar, he replaced the cement bags. *He needs watching. I can't go back to Riverdale until he finishes the landscape job here."*

Irving phoned me. "Are you afraid to come to New York, Maxine?"

"No. I have business in San Diego that I must attend to first. Goodbye."

A week later he phoned, "Maxine, have you changed your mind about divorcing me?"

"Irving, what are you offering me? Why would I change my mind?"

"So, you don't love me anymore, Maxine.'

"Irving, I don't love you any less. However, the landscaper I hired is a thief and needs my constant watching until the job is finished."

"So, your house is more important to you than I am?"

"Irving, a relationship is between people."

"Goodbye, Maxine."

***

It took two months for the landscaping to be done properly. I was very pleased with the job. I was convinced that my house was a lucky buy. I'd purchased it at a very low price, and good fortune had taken care of some of the big expenditures that the house required. I was proud of the house and of myself.

Moreover, I'd made friends with my new neighbors. I was happy to be living in Rancho Bernardo. I was now ready to return to Riverdale and confront Irving. I phoned to tell him that I was coming to New York. It had been fifteen months since I left New York.

He didn't bother to ask me my flight or offer to meet me at the airport. I wondered if I should stay at a friend's house, or take the shuttle to Riverdale.

Rose Epstein was a friend that I'd made while campaigning for Stanley Simon when he ran for Councilman. I recalled that she was a Judge in the family court. I hadn't yet spoken with a lawyer. I thought that she would be the ideal person for me to meet with.

Rose offered to meet me at the airport, and insisted that I come to her house for dinner. We spoke about mutual friends who'd recently moved to retire in other states. Then, I told her how happy I was to have found Rancho Bernardo. I invited her to come and stay with me.

"Maxine, you should consult with your husband before you invite me to come?"

Sigh. "Rose he won't care. My husband says that he wants to divorce me."

"Oh. Did you fool around? You've been gone a long time and we ladies have been wondering what you were doing."

"Irving resents that I bought a house for our retirement."

"That is not grounds for a divorce."

"I resent that I do not have a husband to live with in San Diego. Irving loves his job and he doesn't want to retire. I live as neither as fish nor fowl. I deserve to be loved. He says that he believes that I love the house more than him."

"He can't name a house as correspondent, Maxine, she giggled. Then, she stopped laughing and said, "However, he can sue you for a divorce on the grounds that you've abandoned him."

"Oh? What do you suggest that I do?"

"If you decide that you want to divorce Irving then go to a California divorce lawyer. You've already established residence there, and California is a community property state."

"I didn't know Irving had grounds for a divorce."

"Maxine, if you're content to live your life here with a workaholic then you may have to let go of your house."

'I bought the house for us to live in when he retires."

"Maxine, he doesn't want to retire. That's what this is all about."

She's right. "Rose, I see things more clearly now. Thank you."

"That's what friends are for my dear. Good luck. Would you like me to drive you to Briar Oaks now?"

"Yes, please."

When I entered the lobby in Riverdale, I saw that it had been redecorated in my absence. Gone were the interesting Indian artifacts. In their place were two gaudy looking modern paintings. I couldn't decide which one I disliked more.

Getting off the elevator, I saw that the rugs had been replaced and the hall repainted. *Change is part of life.*

I entered the apartment and heard Irving snoring in the bedroom. *He needs his rest. Tomorrow is a workday.* I'll speak with him tomorrow night.

In the morning, I saw that Irving had left without disturbing me. There was a note on his made bed. "Thanks for not waking me up last night. I'll take you to Stella d' Oro tonight. Love, Irving"

I phoned Natalie, my Brandeis friend and learned there was a luncheon today and a guest speaker was scheduled at The Plaza Hotel.

My first thought was to decline her offer and unpack, but then I thought, perhaps I won't want to stay here after I speak with my husband. *Why go to the trouble of packing twice?*

"What time is it scheduled for, Nat?"

"One o' clock. Want to drive down with me?"

"Sure. Pick me up in an hour, please."

Before we reached the George Washington Bridge, she'd filled me in on the latest gossip in our group of friends. Then, she asked me, "Are you here to stay Maxi?"

"I'm hoping to get Irving to come out west."

"She gave me a sidewise glance, "When you filled in for Irving after his operation didn't you tell me there were scantily clad models walking around the office? You expect him to leave that?"

"We'll see."

Isaac Singer's daughter was the guest speaker. It was amusing when she told the story about her father talking to his friend while they walked and stood at a corner and waited for a signal light to change.

When it did, an impatient woman behind him said, "The light says go!" and he'd replied, "Madam, it's only a suggestion."

I was in a good mood when Irving arrived. He kissed me "Hello." He still loves me. "It's good to see you here where you belong. Maxine." Hmm.

At dinner he asked, "Have you made arrangements yet to sell the house?"
"No. I like the house even more now that the repairs have been done to it. It's really beautiful. You'll enjoy living in it when you retire."

"I'm not planning to retire at any time soon."

"Irving, I don't want to sell the house."

His face turned red, "You like it more than you love me! I want you to sell the house."

"I'm not asking you to retire. It's only a suggestion, Irving. Yet you're asking me to get rid of something that I've worked hard to get into good shape. I don't consider that fair."

"So, you're not staying here, and you do want a divorce."

"I don't think that those are our only options, Irving."

"You'll do it my way, or you can take the highway!"

Other diners in the restaurant turned to stared at us. We both felt embarrassed and left. We didn't attempt to speak to one another even after we got home.

In the morning, I arranged for Federal Express to pick up my packages. Then, I walked to get some large boxes from the supermarket and I took a cab back home. I packed all of my paintings before FedEx arrived. I sent everything back to Rancho Bernardo.

After that, I called for the shuttle and went to the airport to return home with my clothes packed into three large suitcases.

Three days passed before I received a phone call from Irving. "Please, don't divorce me, Maxine. I can't live without you. Take me back."

"You're most welcome to come here, Irving."

"I'm going to speak to Burt tomorrow. I'll convince him that I should sell his merchandise on the west coast."

"That's a brilliant idea Irving, my darling. I knew that you'd figure out a good solution for us both." *Genius ideas are born in despair.*

I was happy to know that we wouldn't be getting a divorce.

CHAPTER 78

In the backyard of my home, I surveyed the garden and trees that had been planted. I smiled. For no particular reason I thought of Mama enduring the cold winter in New York City. Long ago, I realized that she had done the best she could. Too bad it couldn't have been better.

I thought that she hadn't been as fortunate as me. *She had made too many poor choices.* While growing up, it had been difficult for me also, still I felt that growing old was a more difficult experience for her.

I was sorry for the lonely old woman. I realized that one day she would need looking after, but I didn't want her to come and live with me. *Happiness can be expanded when it's shared but not when it's divided.*

I heard about the California Ombudsman organization. It was created to oversee that senior-citizens received good and respectful care in retirement homes, and at assisted living places. So, I volunteered my services while I sought a good place for my mother to live when I brought her out to California.

Meanwhile, mother had contacted my oldest daughter, and she was assisting her grandma. My mother was very happy about this, and not interested in moving to California or in being placed in a retirement home.

I felt somewhat relieved that she didn't want to change her way of living. *Let sleeping dogs lie.*

When it became necessary for my mother to go into an assisted living facility. My daughter selected one near her home. Despite Mama's protests she was placed in it. She loved it, and said she was sorry that she'd fought the idea of entering a retirement place for so long.

Meanwhile, Irving had come out west to open new accounts for his firm. He loved to sun himself in our backyard when he came home from working. He joined a group of men to play cards at the Seven Oaks clubhouse.

He went fishing with one of them, and enjoyed it. He'd never had the opportunity to try it when he was growing up.

We went for walks, played tennis, and went to restaurants with our new friends. Now, Irving went to work only when he wasn't meeting with his buddies.

***

The nation was in an economic slump, and Irving didn't get reorders on the accounts that he'd opened. I was concerned because achieving sales was important to him. However, he smiled and said, "It's time for me to retire. I was worried that there' d be nothing for me to do each day when I stopped working."

He laughed, "Maxine, retirement is the best job I ever had."

I didn't say anything and put my arms around Irving and kissed him.

Several months later, I returned home and was surprised to see Irving with his head swathed in bandages. "What happened to you, Irving?"

Sheepishly, he grinned, "I guess I fell asleep while I was driving home. I woke up on a neighbor's lawn after I hit his tree."

"Who else was hurt?"

"No. one It was only the tree, the car, and I. The policeman took away my driver's license at the hospital. Maxine, please get it back for me. I need it."

He shouldn't be behind the wheel of a car if he falls asleep. "Irving, what did the doctor say to you?"

"Oh, I'm all right. I should get more sleep at night."

More sleep? He sleeps fourteen hours a day, and takes naps. "Did you see your doctor or the Emergency Room doctor?"

"The ER Doctor."

"Irving, I'm going to make an appointment for you with your doctor."

"Why? I feel all right."

"It will make me feel better."

"Okay."

CHAPTER 79

"Mrs. Feller, I'm sorry to tell you that your husband has senior dementia."

"Is that the same as Alzheimers?"

"Frankly, it's the beginning stages of it. However, I'm not entering that on his medical record because it will make it harder for you to place him in a retirement home."

"Should he ever be allowed to drive?"

"I don't think that's a good idea. I will prescribe a drug that should delay the progress of the disease. You will find him relying on you more and more as he experiences these episodes. Otherwise, he's in excellent health."

There's no need to tell the children yet. I'll ask them to send us more photos, and plan to spend time with us as soon as soon as possible. I'm glad that my Ombudsman experience will come in handy.

I phoned my daughter, and learned that my mother's health was failing. She was too busy with her family to come out to visit any time soon. Her news further distressed me. I considered going to New York but I had a bad head cold and flying would be very painful. It was more important for me to be a good wife and stay with my husband than fly to New York to say "Goodbye" to my mother.

I was sorry that I wouldn't get to see her before she died, but my husband was my first priority and there was no one else to look after him.

Several weeks later, my husband was still badgering me for his driver's license. I said, "Irving, I don't have the power to give it to you. If you want to drive then take the driver's test. After you pass it, they must give it to you." *It would be better if he fought with someone other than me.*

"Yes. You're right, Maxine. I'll do that."

He smiled when I gave him the phone book to select a driving school. I made arrangements for him to attend. *Whew. He was no longer angry with me. Why didn't I think of this sooner?*

Irving became much more pleasant to live with. Being a caretaker is not an easy task. He extolled the virtues of his pretty teacher after each lesson. *I was well aware that she would soon be referred to as "the bitch that kept him from driving". Better her than me.*

I continued my search to find him a nice and affordable retirement place. After dinner, we would play gin rummy. It was sad to know that our days of pleasant interaction were coming to an inevitable end. *I studied his dear face and mannerisms when he won or lost a game. It was hard for me not to cry.*

I missed him already. I realized that I had to plan for life without him. I didn't stop seeing my friends, but I devoted most of my time to staying at home with him. I was afraid that if I dropped out of all my activities, I would lose my friends after Irving was no longer with me.

I hired a local cab driver to take Irving to his buddies to play cards and "shoot the breeze" while I was involved in other activities. To outsiders it appeared that we were living a normal life. Slowly, I saw that my husband was slipping away from me as he became more and more forgetful. I didn't want us to part, and overlooked a lot of things that he did.

One afternoon, I returned and he told me that a nice lady had driven him home after his friends had refused to play cards with him anymore.

He sobbed, "They told me not to come back". *They must be seeing what I don't want to see.* I knew the time was close when he'd need to go into a retirement facility. I cancelled the cab service, and stayed home with him.

One day, he wanted me to make fish cakes for his lunch, but I was out of breadcrumbs. I told Irving that I'd be right back, and drove to the grocer to get a new box.

When I returned, he wasn't in the house or backyard. *Where can he be?*

I knocked on the doors of neighbors and enlisted their help looking for him. We searched the neighborhood. One of the men found Irving weeping on a curb twelve blocks away.

He sobbed to me, "I went looking for you, Maxine. Then, I forgot how to get home." He was very upset, and it took me a few hours to calm him down.

After I made him lunch, I phoned the retirement home that I'd decided to use. I was told they would send out an "intake nurse" to my home. The doorbell rang, and Irving opened the door.

He said, "Well, hello there. I'm glad you came to visit me." I was very surprised that he knew her. "Maxine, this is that nice lady that I told you about who drove me home last week."

I thought, "What a wonderful coincidence" and invited her to come in.

During the friendly conversation with the woman, her name was "Apple", she happened to mention that a couple planning to live at the facility had decided to go and live nearer to their children. *This is the hand of Providence at work here I thought.*

Quickly I said, "Irving, let's go and see the place. I'll take your bag along with us in case you like it."

This was a gentle way to get him to leave the house, and go to visit the retirement facility. I'd been dreading telling Irving that it would be safer for him to live where he'd never be left alone again and there would be a gate to keep him from wandering away. I didn't want to put either of us through that awful experience again.

The Nightingale Home was clean and charming. It had a locked gate. So, I didn't bother to mention to them that Irving had wandered off before I had called them.

The large sunny room Apple showed us had a double brass bed, and a Victorian dresser and other furniture that made it look very homey. It was unlike the dreary hospital looking institutions that I'd seen.

I considered, *They want this expensive room rented quickly. I was delighted with the place, and ready to sign him in immediately.*

Apple hadn't had the opportunity to administer any tests to Irving yet she was carried along with the flow of coincidence and mutual need. She gave her approval for Irving to be admitted. I signed the contract. I was relieved that everyone was happy to be getting what it was they needed. I visited my husband each day.

I brought photographs to him to place around the room, and recent ones that the children had sent me. Irving often spoke about his pretty night nurse, but he didn't want to make friends with the other residents.

CHAPTER 80

I saw that Irving was losing weight. "Don't you like the food they serve you here?"

"It isn't that, Maxine. After a few bites, I just don't want to eat any more." I decided to feed my husband. However, I saw that he would eat just to please me, but he didn't want to eat even half of the food on his plate.

I went to speak with the doctor at the facility who assured me that my husband was in good health. "It's common for the elderly to eat less and less."

With his permission, I purchased my husband a basketball for Irving and had a hoop installed. I thought that less television and more exercise might help increase Irving's appetite. He enjoyed tossing the ball and being out in the sunshine, but it didn't increase his appetite.

Several weeks later, Irving was startled when I entered his room. He doesn't know me. I was upset and hurt. "How can my husband of nearly fifty years not know me?"

Then, I became angry. Why should I bother to come here if Irving doesn't know me?

After services on Friday night, I spoke with my Rabbi. She said, "Didn't you once tell me that Irving had senior dementia and that was the start of

Alzheimer?"

"Yes, Rabbi."

"Well, Maxine it's his disease that doesn't know you, and not your husband."

"How can I relate to a stranger living in my husband's body?"

"I don't know, but it's not with anger. Your husband has lost the wonderful memories you both once shared. He must be very lonely now."

The following day, when I visited Irving, I knocked on the closed door, and waited for him to say, "Come in."

He was seated at the balcony door looking out at the trees. "Isn't it a nice day, Irving?"

"Oh, do you know me? I'm sorry but I don't remember your name."

"It's Maxine. We were once very good friends."

"Thank you for coming to see me, Maxine."

"Is there anything that you'd like me to do for you?"

"No. Thank you. What did you say your name is?"

"Irving, look at the little brown bird on the tree. I think he's starting to build a nest in its branches."

"I like to watch birds too."

He was no longer my Irving, but he's a nice person. I sat next to him for a few minutes until he fell asleep. Then I left.

***

I was awakened by a phone call from the nursing home. "The doctor has just sent Mr. Feller to the hospital by ambulance."

I dressed and rushed to the hospital. Irving had been admitted, and was resting in a private room. I was allowed to go in and see him. He appeared to be asleep. I heard him cry out, "Mama". Then, I held his hand in mine.

Irving opened his eyes and saw me. He looked frightened, and pulled his hand away. I asked softly, "Irving, would you like something to drink?"

He nodded, and I held a straw in the water glass beside the bed. I placed it between his lips. He sipped then sighed, and closed his eyes.

I sat and dozed beside my husband until the nurse came into the room. She took Irving's pulse then phoned for the doctor. Within minutes, the doctor entered the room. He examined my husband and said, "I'm sorry. He's gone."

Next, he pulled the sheet up over him. I burst into tears and sobbed, "My life is over. I'm an orphan and a widow."

The nurse hushed me and said, "There are patients asleep on this floor. Then, she came over to hold me in her outstretched arms.

"You're still a young woman. You'll find another man to love". She then told me that there were papers to sign. I sighed and wiped away my tears. I walked to the nurse's station and signed the necessary papers.

A nurse's aide handed me an envelope. I opened it and saw it contained my husband's sweater and teeth, and his watch.

I felt numb as I waited for the elevator to take me to the lobby. Outside, the moon and stars shone brightly. A cool wind brushed my face and I shivered.

Recalling the sweater inside the envelope, I reached in to get it. I slipped it on. I dropped his teeth into the nearest trashcan, and walked to my car.

I remained seated behind the wheel until the sun came up. A security guard saw me, and asked if I was all right. I nodded and then drove home.

After that, I phoned the children. No one was available to sit shiva with me. I didn't want to be alone.

I went to my writing group. My friends commented that I didn't look well. I followed their suggestion that I go see my doctor. He told me I had an e-coli infection and put me on antibiotics. I stayed at home and rested until the doctor said that I was "okay".

Mechanically, I did all the things that a widow needs to do. I was glad that I had moved to California and had made my own friends long before Irving came out west. In Riverdale, I'd observed that the so called married friends remained friends with the widow. *Did those insecure wives fear losing their husbands to a single woman in the group? Would that happen in California?*

After several weeks, the husbands of my girlfriends came one by one to "console" me. I soon realized that those "Good Samaritans" weren't interested in only consoling me. I rebuffed their unwanted advances.

Although I never informed on them to their wives, it felt awkward to be in their homes. I arranged to meet the ladies at the clubhouse for bridge or have lunch in with them in various restaurants.

I was all right during the day. However, at about 5:30, loneliness set in and I lost all my energy, which made me feel tired and uneasy.

I decided to join an evening aerobic class at one of the pools. I needed exercise, and it would fill the hours that I found so difficult. Also, it gave me the opportunity to make other friends.

I was reluctant to be seen in my old bathing suit, I was always the last one to enter the pool. It was more like dancing than exercise, and I loved doing it. When the class ended, I hurried to the showers. As I waited my turn, I was invited by one of the women on the line to join her at the coffee shop for a snack.

I hadn't eaten dinner and I was ravenous. She nibbled at her salad while I enjoyed my Denver omelet.

"My name is Loretta," she said with an interesting accent. "My friends call me Lala. What's there to do around here for fun?"

We could go to a late movie."

"I feel too invigorated to sit still."

"Is your accent British?"

"No. Australian."

"Want to go for a walk in the park?"

"Isn't there a roadhouse somewhere for us to go dancing?"

"I don't know of any."

"Don't they have dances in this town?"

"Sure. Monday afternoons at the Senior Center."

"Would you go there with me?"

"I volunteer at the hospital, but I can meet you there afterwards."

"Is this Monday okay, Maxine?"

"All right, Lala."

CHAPTER 81

The auditorium was dimly lit. The live band was playing when I arrived at the dance. A rotating mirrored ball on the ceiling helped to create the illusion of a ballroom. I saw Lala wearing an iridescent low-cut dress on the dance floor. She appeared to be glued to a much younger man.

When she saw me, she pulled away from him, and hurried over to me.

"Maxine, is your place nearby?" I could smell alcohol on her breath and asked, "Are you feeling all right, Lala?"

"May I borrow your bedroom for a few hours?"

"You'll be okay. I'll get you some black coffee."

"You don't understand, Maxine. I met someone I really like. I want to see where it leads us."

"Not to my bedroom. Take him to your own house."

"My husband is there. Are you just another jealous prude?"

"Lala, you may do whatever you please, but not in my home. Excuse me, there's a friend I want to see. "Goodbye, Lala forgot that you know me."

I quickly walked away. I took a seat near the bandstand, but no one asked me to dance. At the music break a man took the seat beside me. He said, "It was elegant the way you said "No" and left her." I turned to him and asked, "Excuse me. What're you talking about?"

"I'm the drummer in the band. I see a lot from up there on the bandstand. When you came into the room I saw a woman with real class. Then, it surprised me to see that bimbo saunter over to speak with you. \

It was no surprise to me that you got rid of her in short order without making a scene."

"Oh that… She mistook me for someone else." *Individual men play music. I'd never thought of the band as anything but music background.*

"What's your name?"

"Maxine Feller."

"Hello Maxine. My name is Bob Howard. After the dance, I'd like to take you out for a cup of coffee."

I saw that he wasn't wearing a wedding ring and I said, "Okay."

After the dance, Bob packed his drums and placed them in the trunk of his blue Ford. I followed him in my car to the mall.

He brought two cups of black coffee back to our table. "I was married forty years to a wonderful woman who insisted on smoking herself to death. Monette was a great cook. I still miss her cooking Tell me about you"

"My husband died several months ago from pneumonia after almost fifty years of a happy marriage. I don't cook but I do make reservations."

"So, you haven't yet really felt the impact of a what it's like to be alone and lonely."

"I'm no stranger to those feelings, Bob."

"Perhaps you're ready to go out with me then?"

"What do you have in mind?"

"Church, lunch, and dancing at the Elk's Lodge."

"Bob, I'm Jewish."

He said: "In World War Two I liberated many Jews from Nazi prison camps. It was dreadful to see what those poor souls went through. If the German soldiers hadn't run-away, I'd have shot them down like dogs."

"So, you're a war hero?"

"I just did my part like everyone else. Maxine, I want you to hear my Priest. He's hilarious. He sprinkles his sermon with funny stories, and only speaks in English." *Listen to a service in a language that I'd be able to understand?* Hmm. "That sounds interesting, Bob."

"Good. I hope that you'll come with me this Sunday. I'm not a great dancer, but many who come to the Elk Dances are professional dancers. We'll enjoy seeing them in action on the dance floor."

When there was slow dance played Bob asked me to dance with him. He said, "I knew that you'd fit perfectly in my arms, Maxine."

Bob was a strong leader and I enjoyed being held in his warm embrace. He told me that he was interested in astronomy. Before the evening ended, he asked me out again, and I accepted. We went to the Planetarium.

On our date he suggested several other things of interest that we could see and do. "Maxine, no one else has been interested in doing the things that I like to do. We're soul mates." I smiled and nodded in agreement.

Bob knew what I wanted before I did. He filled the deep loneliness that I'd felt after Irving died with his warmth and presence.

It came as no surprise three months later when Bob told me that he loved me as we sat smooching in my living room. He asked me to marry him.

I replied, "We do well together, Bob. Let's live together first, and then we'll see if we still want to marry." *Why ruin a good friendship with marriage.*

"No, Maxine. I love you too much for that. I won't have your neighbors gossiping about you behind your back."

He's more highly principled than I am. He cares more about what other people think of me than I do. Bob must really love me.

"This is so sudden, Bob. You must realize that I'll need time to think it over. *What will my children say when they hear I'm thinking about re-marriage to someone that isn't Jewish?*

"You know that I love you, Maxine. We're soul mates. If you want to throw away our chance at happiness then I'll accept your decision. I won't call you for two weeks. If you don't call me, then I won't be seeing you again. *He means all or nothing.*

Bob gave me a long farewell kiss that sent chills up and down my spine and made me want him. My heart beat faster, "Don't go. Kiss me more." I said, but he left.

CHAPTER 82

Over the next few days I considered the facts of my life carefully. I'm a widow who gets my husband's Social Security benefits. If I will marry again, do I lose that income? Will my children think that I didn't love their father if I remarry?

I didn't want to deprive my children of my husband's estate that I worked so hard to create. Yet, I felt entitled to have a companion and enjoy my life to the fullest. Did I want to return to my lonely widow's existence?

I figured I had more money than Bob. *Is he more interested in what I have than being with me?*

My friends had all accepted Bob yet advised me to wait until I knew him better. *Act in haste repent at leisure.*

My children said they had been concerned about me living alone. They approved of me having a companion who had lifted me out of the doldrums after their father died. They liked the idea that I wanted to lead a life of mine own.

Social Security assured me that I would not lose my widow benefits. I missed Bob's entertaining phone calls each day, and being held in his arms, and excited by his kisses.

The quiet of my house got on my nerves. I was aware something was missing, and I could easily have it again in my life. My Rabbi said she wouldn't marry us unless he converted to Judaism. I didn't want to marry in his church. Bottom line…I did want Bob Howard to be in my life.

I phoned him a few days before the two weeks were up. He asked, "What took you so long to call me?"

"There were things I had to think through."

"Like?"

"If we're going to split our bills, are you earning enough money to cover your share?"

"Monette's illness and hospital bills did pretty much wipe me out. However, I do own my condominium in Bernardo Heights free and clear. Also, I do two or three gigs each month.

"Well then, I suggest that we live in my house and you can rent out your condo to cover your share of our bills."

"That's a great idea, Maxine. I'll put your name on the title to the condo. Are you busy today?"

"Never too busy to see you, Bob."

"It's good to hear you say that. I'll come right over to pick you up, and we'll drive downtown to get it done today."

After we'd filled out the forms and signed the papers to change the title, I felt awkward asking Bob to sign a Pre-nuptial agreement that my lawyer and I had drawn up before I'd phoned him. He read it with interest and signed without hesitation.

My friend offered me the use of her home and garden when I set the date to marry Bob. I replaced several of her plants, landscaped the hedges, and trees for the occasion.

On the day of the wedding, Bob selected the best musicians in San Diego to play. Bob was childless. His nephew and his wife and several cousins came to our wedding feast.

My dear friend, Dori didn't like Bob, but offered to arrange for the Caterer. George, her husband became a certified minister to be able to perform my marriage to Bob. *Chosen friends make the best family.*

All my children and lovely grandchildren attended our beautiful wedding ceremony. Also, my single friends and close neighbors attended. The weather was perfect.

After the ceremony, a mishap occurred when my Florida born southern husband saw David, a Negro friend assisting my daughter with her children seated at their table. Bob had to be restrained by his nephew and others from trying to eject David off the premises.

I was embarrassed by Bob's behavior and apologized to David. Then, Bob became furious with me for being polite to David, and apologizing for his actions to a "nigger."

"I wondered why it hadn't occurred to me that some southerners are known to be bigots. This was a side of Bob that I had never seen. Over the weekend, I helped Bob pack up some things he wanted to bring to my house, or put into storage before he rented out his condo.

In a closet, I came across a photo of Bob with his Navy buddies. *How could he have liberated Jews in Germany if he wasn't even in the army? Why had he lied to me?* I didn't confront him with the photograph. *I fight to win something. I don't fight battles that lead nowhere. Let sleeping dogs lie.* Bob would probably deny that he'd said it.

After a game of tennis with Dori, I discussed my discovery with her. She asked, "Maxine, what advantage did Bob gain with you by making up that story?"

"I liked that he'd done it and was sympathetic to the victims of the Nazis."

"Aren't southerners renowned Negro and Jew haters?"

"That's what I've heard about some of them."

"So by telling you that lie he disassociated himself from them, you saw him in a different light?"

"I don't know that I'd have thought about whether or not he liked Jews. The first date we had, I told Bob that I was Jewish when he asked me to go to Church with him. It's just weird."

"I think that you were smart not to confront him about it, Maxine. It probably would've made him angry to be caught in a lie."

"Yes. That's what I'd suspected too. No sense having an argument where nobody wins.

"Maxine, did Jeanne tell you what Bob said to her husband after he explained to you how to use a change of date to retrieve lost material on your computer?"

"Jeannie said she had an early tennis match. So, they had to leave early. Was there any more to it than that?"

"I happened to overhear your husband order Chuck out of the house when you went into the kitchen to get more burritos."

"What? He ordered one of my friends out of my house? Now that's something I will talk to Bob about."

Dori had once told me that she didn't like Bob. *If I hadn't seen proof that Bob tells lies I'd have doubted what she told me.* I intended to check out the incident. I would talk to Bob, and tell him not to do it again as soon as I got home.

Bob was slumped in a living room chair gasping for air when I returned home. He gasped, "Get me to Scripps Emergency."

I ran to get John, my neighbor around the corner to help me put Bob into my car. I took his medications with us and drove to the hospital.

They quickly attended to him. The doctor told me that he'd had a panic attack and suggested that Bob remain overnight.

I left and stopped by to thank John for his help. I told him that Bob was all right. Ruth asked me to stay to discuss something important.

"We've been friends a long time, Maxine and our neighbors know that. Recently, I was surprised when asked by some of them if they'd offended you in any way. They told me that Bob had said you felt offended by them, and no longer wanted to be friends with them.

They're wondering what they might've done to offend you, and asked me if I knew what it was that they had done."

"Ruth, I can't imagine why Bob said such a thing. No one has done anything to hurt my feelings. Please, tell them that."

Then, I told Ruth and John about finding the photo of Bob and his Navy buddies after he'd told me that he'd liberated Jews from prison camps when he was in the Army.

We were puzzled. John suggested that I discuss the strange goings on with Bob's doctor.

Bob's doctor told me that he'd been treating Bob for a very long time. He knew that Bob had a quick temper, a "vivid imagination, and a need for adulation. He had prescribed medications to help him with these issues.

I asked, "Doctor, are you also a psychiatrist?" Embarrassed, he turned red and said, "I see your point, Mrs. Howard. I'll insist that Bob gets a second opinion for this recent attack. Then, I'll send him to someone qualified to assess his current mental state."

When Bob left the hospital, he insisted on driving downtown to San Diego. He pointed out all the places that he had lived, before he brought his wife to San Diego.

"Why did you move so frequently, Bob?"

He gave me a sidewise glance and replied, "Simple. I didn't want the girls to know where to find me."

The following day, I drove Bob to see the Psychiatrist. He interviewed both of us, then Bob, and then me. "Like all men of this kind he appears to be very charming, and lovable."

"Does he love me? Is he happy with me?"

"Are you happy with him?"

"I thought I was until I discovered that he wasn't the man I thought I had married."

Bob agreed to schedule additional appointments with this doctor but this time without me, as the Doctor had suggested

Two weeks later, Bob asked me for a divorce. I suggested that we try going to a marriage counselor.

"No. I've been that route. It doesn't work." I didn't bother to argue with him.

Dori drove me to each meeting with my divorce lawyer. She was a pillar of strength for me.

Bob moved back into his condo and his solicitous female neighbors.

I was amazed when he called to ask me to go out with him several times. I told him, "Let's wait until after we're divorced."

Two of my three children had been divorced, and I no longer felt it was shameful to divorce.

My lawyer commented that he'd never seen a client recover from the trauma of divorce as quickly as I had. I didn't grieve over my divorce. Thanks to Bob I had been released from the depression of widowhood. I no longer grieved for my Irving, or our way of life before he'd died.

Alone again, I felt free to meet and enjoy each day. My friends encouraged me to go with them to Alaska. When I returned from the cruise, I volunteered at the Rancho Bernardo Public Library.

Everyone was learning to use a computer. One of the volunteers told me that she'd spent many interesting afternoons having coffee with men that she'd "met on the internet."

So, I thought: *Why not give it a try?*

The first fellow I met seemed like an interesting person. He suggested that we have breakfast at an "IHOP" restaurant in Vista.

He was a widower, had been in the Navy and loved to play golf. There was a miniature golf course that I had taken my grandchildren to when they'd visited me. It was close to this restaurant, and I suggested that we go there.

I was glad that we were getting to know one another. I confessed that I rarely played golf, but that I was happy to try it.

He bragged that he shot in the low eighties. *I didn't know whether or not that was a good score.* We obtained the balls and clubs from the cashier, and went on to hole one.

He said, "Ladies first". I placed my ball on the ground and swung. To my surprise I shot a hole in one on my first try.

It took him twelve strokes to sink the ball. Each time he tried to hit it, his face became redder and redder. By the time the ball finally dropped into the hole, I thought I could see steam coming out of his ears. I was careful not to laugh and had to turn away several times. Then, we proceeded to the next hole.

He was much better after that first hole and I became progressively worse. *If this man is so upset about his playing, then he takes himself too seriously.* I thought he didn't have the right attitude to learn from his mistakes, to just laugh and to try again. So, I didn't accept when he asked me to go out with him again.

After that, I dated a self-important man who drove a Land Rover; then a fellow who drove a yellow Corvette and was a hero in his own eyes.

After several more disappointing dates, I was ready to give up computer dating. However, I noticed the photograph of a pleasant looking man. Hmm.

Perhaps I would have more in common with him than I had had with those other men.

I contacted Irwin. He did not want to settle for a coffee date. *I'd lost two pounds and was afraid of the temptation of good food.* He suggested that we have dinner Saturday night at his favorite Italian restaurant. It was Joe's Italian Diner in Escondido.

I telephoned my daughter to wish her a Happy Birthday before I left to meet Irwin. She was born on the same day (September 28) that I met Irving. It was an important date to me, and I was glad that I wouldn't be celebrating it by myself.

As I drove toward Escondido to meet Irwin, I thought about the day that I met my husband. It had been a chance meeting yet things went so smoothly we'd both felt that our meeting had been pre-destined.

Irving proposed to me on our third date. I smiled when I recalled that I told him that I didn't know him well enough to say "Yes" or "No." *Yet I knew that I felt at ease with him, and wanted to continue to see him.*

How would tonight's date turn out? I arrived promptly at six at "Joe's", and found a parking space on the same street. A waiter met me at the door when I entered. "Is there a gentleman here by the name of Irwin Schenker.

"He hasn't arrived yet. Please follow me" and he led me to a booth that allowed me to see whoever entered the restaurant. "May I bring you a glass of wine or a coffee?"

"Thank you. A red wine would be nice". He brought me a glass. The door opened and several people entered. He left me and hurried over to greet them. I took a sip of wine and started to wonder if I'd been stood up.

Then, the front door opened and I recognized Irwin's face. He saw me seated alone and hurried toward me, "Hello. I hope that you're Maxine?"

I smiled and extended my hand for him to shake, "You're late."

"I was looking for a place to park. It won't happen again"

The waiter brought us our menus, "I entertained your lady while she was waiting for you." he said. Irwin remarked that the veal picata was excellent here.

"That's what I'll have."

"It's my favorite dish too. They make it great here. I'm sure that you will enjoy it.

We continued to talk until eight o' clock. Then, Irwin paid the bill and we walked to my car. *We talked some more until my feet hurt from standing there so long in my high heels.*

I said: "Thank you for a delicious dinner, and a very pleasant evening."

"I had a great time too." He asked me for my phone number, and I gave it to him. Irwin was a "mench", but he enjoyed his food too much. It was clear to me that if I continued to go out with him, I'd was sure that I would regain the weight that I had lost. I liked eating good food too. I had dieted strenuously to lose the two pounds and to prepare myself before Irwin called me for another date.

When he did phone, I had lost only one pound. I suggested that we go to a movie, and have a light bite afterwards. He agreed.

After the movie we had coffee and chocolate pie. I nibbled at mine, and he finished it for me.

Later, Irwin told me that he was a diabetic. I was horrified that I'd let him finish my pie. *Neither of us needed to eat pie.* I realized it would've been healthier to eat a light meal before we saw the show.

My friend Kathy was losing her husband to diabetes one limb at a time. *It was dreadful to see less and less of him.*

I liked Irwin more each time we met. I couldn't bear seeing that happen to him. *The fact that he was a diabetic discouraged me from thinking seriously about him.*

I decided to stop seeing him before I didn't want to stop seeing him. He phoned and I told him, "Irwin, I don't think we're right for one another. I'm not going to see you anymore." "Will you talk to me if I call you?" "Yes, of course.

"Then, why won't you see me?" The doorbell rang!

"My doorbell is ringing incessantly", I said, "I have to hang up." I hurried to the door. The block captain was standing on the doorstep. He told me that there was a serious fire heading in our direction from Witch Creek, and advised me to pack what I needed to take with me before the alarm to evacuate the area came.

Dori and I had planned to go to Solvang for the weekend. My clothes were already packed. So, I put my precious photos in a box. Then, I gathered up my jewelry and my oil paintings and took them out to my car. I phoned Dori.

There was no answer. The doorbell rang and I hurried to open it. It was Dori. "Jo Ann said it was all right for me to come over. All of Rancho Bernardo is leaving! Let's get out of here!"

I got into my car and followed Dori to the Highway. I saw that the North bound entrance was closed and blocked by a police car. *No chance of us going to Solvang.*

The Southbound entrance was still open, and we drove through the haze of smoke to Jo Ann's home while we were still able to use the Highway.

It was twilight when we arrived in Mira Mesa and parked outside of Jo Ann's house. I parked next to Dori's car. Leaving my valuables in the car, I removed my overnight bag from the trunk.

Entering the dimly lit house, I overheard Jo Ann complaining that there wasn't enough room for another guest.

It was dark and this was my first time in her new home. I didn't realize that her home had a step-down living room. Wham! I found myself sprawled out on the living room floor. I was stunned. My ankle hurt.

Jo Ann and Dori must've heard me scream when I fell. They arrived armed with frozen peas and an ice bag. *If I hadn't fallen and hurt myself, I would've driven to a hotel in downtown San Diego.*

Jo Ann was a chiropractor, and immediately set to work on my injured ankle and calf. She told me not to put any weight on my ankle, and insisted I that I sleep downstairs on the rug, or the couch. I apologized for my clumsiness and thanked her for her hospitality. She gave me an Excedrin PM and a muscle relaxant.

In the morning the swelling had subsided somewhat. However, my ankle still throbbed and pained me. She worked her magic on my leg, and the pain eased.

"Jo Ann, if it was meant for me to fall anywhere, I'm glad that it was with you nearby. Thank you." She told me to stay off my leg for another day.

We watched television and saw the terrible devastation from the raging fire which still was not under control. Two of our San Diego fire crews had been sent to Los Angeles to fight the forest fires up north. They couldn't come back until the fires were contained. What a mess!

My cell phone rang and I answered it, "Hello". It was Irwin in Oceanside. He was concerned about me, and offered me the hospitality of his home. *I didn't feel that I should take advantage of his offer.* "Thank you for your offer Irwin, but I'm safe here in Mira Mesa. I'm staying with friends. Thanks for calling me. I'll phone you when I get back home."

I was touched by his genuine concern and generosity. *Irwin is a good man and worthy of my love.* I'd been hasty and foolish to allow my lack of self-discipline to dictate that I shouldn't see him anymore.

The next morning, Jo Ann received a phone call ordering her to evacuate her house. The wind had changed and the fire was quickly advancing this way. I felt in a panic. *Would there be room for me in the next place she went to?*

My cell phone rang and I answered. Irwin demanded, "Maxine come at once. North of Highway 15 is open for now." He then gave me directions and repeated: "come now."

I breathed a sigh of relief and uttered: "Thank you."

Jo Ann was relieved when I told her that I was leaving to go to Oceanside. We three hugged, and I left.

It was painful to drive yet I managed to get there with the help of my Mercedes governor. Irwin was a gracious host. There was a bedroom for me upstairs. I didn't tell him that I'd fallen. I asked him for an ice pack. *He didn't need to know that I was a klutz.* He brought it up to me along with a glass of water and an aspirin. I placed the ice pack on my ankle.

Seated comfortably on his couch, we watched the progress of the Witch Creek fire. *Whew... I was glad to be safe with Irwin's at my side.* He took my hand, and I smiled at him. *I knew that he was concerned for my welfare. That had ignited a spark in my heart.* It felt good to feel wanted and safe in this gated Oceanside community with Irwin. He wanted an amiable companion, and so did I.

Being the fifth wheel even if you're the parent is still being the fifth, and it feels awkward. Neither of us wanted to let go past memories of our loved ones. Irwin was my escort to Bar Mitzvas, weddings, engagements and reunions. We traveled the world as a couple for many years. It was pleasant for both of us. *I trusted him completely.*

Then, he stopped attending the "Boys Brunch" Friday mornings. After that, he started to repeat his sentences, and became forgetful. Then, he had an attack and I drove him to the hospital immediately.

It was a mild heart attack the doctor said, Then, he informed me he 'd found Irwin had senior dementia. I told his son when we went to spend the weekend at his home. He didn't believe me. And when I suggested he locate a facility nearby he got angry with me.

Living in Oceanside with Irwin had been pleasant for both of us, but I wasn't his wife and it wasn't my place to seek out a place where he would need to go one day. So, I talked things over with my friend Dori.

"Like it or not the handwriting is on the wall" she said.

I had sold my house in Rancho Bernardo. Where was I to go? I was thinking about it when Irwin came into the kitchen and announced, "Maxine, you're going to die before me."

What nonsense are you talking…you're not funny Irwin. You're the one who just had a heart attack and not me. What makes you think I'm going to die before you?

Come into the bedroom and I'll show you, and I followed him. Then, he opened a dresser drawer and pulled out a box with a beautiful Bowie knife in it.

I thought it was a new trophy to add to the gun collection that hung on the wall behind his desk, and said, "What a beautiful knife you have." Then he put the knife back in the box and closed the drawer.

The oven alarm went off and we went back to the kitchen to eat the roast I had baked for our dinner.

After dinner I was at the sink washing the dishes when I nicked my finger. I saw my blood run down the sink and thought about what Irwin had said earlier. Was he joking? It wasn't like him to tease me. I decided to go back and remove the knife from the drawer and put it elsewhere until I spoke with his doctor.

I became frightened when I found the box was no longer in the drawer. I called Dori…

"Maxine, you get out of the house and come here right now."

I used my cell phone to call the house, and hurried into the kitchen to answer the phone. I pretended I was talking to Dori then hung up.

After that, I told Irwin I was going out to see Dori, and I wouldn't be long. He voiced no objection and I left the house. Once behind the wheel of my car I stopped trembling. If the knife had still been in the drawer, would I be scared now/

Irving had been ill a long time, but he had never threatened me. I was never scared of him…and I had to admit I no longer felt I could trust Irwin…and I was afraid of him.

At the intersection ahead on this two-lane street I saw an out of state car. I saw the traffic light would soon change and I beeped the horn to signal the car to move to the curb and let me pass. I figured the driver was lost. However, the car didn't move and I pulled a sharp left to go around the stopped car and make the light. I'd forgotten the dealer had talked me into a Mercedes sports car when I recently traded in my 320 Sedan.

And to my surprise my car didn't go around the car but headed straight to the curb and the car was suddenly air borne. I heard the air bags inflate… When I opened my eyes, I didn't see any inflated air bags around me—-a policeman was rapping on my window and indicated I should open the door…but I found I couldn't move my left arm. So, I reached over with my right hand to unlock the door.

The officer asked if I had my seat belt on, and I told him yes. He released it and asked me to step out of the car. An ambulance came and I found I was unable to move my right leg. The ambulance men got me out and I insisted they take me to my doctor's hospital, and not the closest one.

I was surprised to see Irwin at the hospital. He told me to give him my rings. I hesitated…Then he said your fingers will swell and they'll have to cut them off… during the operation…and then I handed him my heirloom marquis shaped marcasite ring with a diamond in its center.

After the surgery, I was sent to a rehab. I was glad I wasn't sent to Irwin's house. I no longer trusted him and wouldn't feel safe alone there with him.

It took me two months of intensive physical therapy to get out of the wheelchair and onto a walker. My daughter volunteered to be with me when I returned to Oceanside, and then I agreed to go back there.

While they loaded the car with my things, I heard my daughter complain that Irwin had almost caught her hand while she put my things in the trunk. He poos pooed the idea, but later I told her I was afraid Irwin wanted to hurt me too.

After two days of near misses, I phoned his son and told him I was concerned about his father having another heart attack while I was unable to care for him.

He came that weekend and took his dad to live with him. Whew.

Naomi graciously invited me to come and live with her. I told her I'd think about it. I enjoyed the weather and activities in this community, but I wasn't sure how I could manage to get around without a car.

Nightly, Irwin would call me. I didn't like playing this insincere telephone game with him for the benefit of his son to hear what a wonderful guy he was to me. We were done. So, I called to thank him for the good years we'd had and tell him I would soon be leaving, and put an end to this charade. It felt good to be honest. Naomi left to take the physical for job she wanted in Texas.

However, on Saturday when my granddaughter and I returned from grocery shopping the key suddenly didn't fit the door. We drove to the gate and was told Irwin's son had entered earlier with a locksmith. I quickly recalled how Irwin had by passed the locks and entered his house, and his method still worked.

On Sunday morning Irwin called to tell me I was trespassing on his property. On Monday morning an officer came to the house to "evict me". I explained the situation to him. He advised me I had a common law partnership since I'd been there more than seven years, and left.

Naomi phoned and asked if breast cancer might be an inherited gene? They'd found a lump in her breast. In a flash my mother instincts bolstered my strength and I felt able to take care of my daughter whether or not she had cancer. And she was happy to hear I had decided to move to Texas to be nearer to her.

My leg was still in a cast but my arm was healed. Kayla got me boxes and then we packed for the movers. What a patient and great helper she was, and a good driver too. From her I learned how to sleep in a car and be a camper, and not be as judgmental as I'd been.

Unfortunately, Naomi's biopsy showed it was cancerous, she researched carefully and selected the right surgeon and hospital, I was happy to be there to help her in any way I could. She married her sweetheart before her operation. Paul is super nice.

He allowed my furniture to be delivered to his spacious home, and invited me to stay there as long as I liked.

However, I wanted to live closer to my grandchildren. Kayla drove me to several senior living communities and I selected one. The day I moved in I was introduced to one of the residents and he and I became good friends. But he monopolized all my time, and I wasn't making girlfriends. Then, one day my exercise class was cancelled and I found Bill in my room. He hadn't taken anything but I decided to move to another facility.

He came to visit me often, and was able to express better his feelings for me. I liked him very much, but not enough to marry him. We had similar interests and often traveled together, and became very good friends.

Also, I had no car and Bill often drove me wherever I wanted to go and patiently waited. Then, he started to have severe back pains due to his kidneys, Bill refused to take dialysis treatments to help his condition, and asked me to come back to live at Provident Crossing Community Resort, and I did.

I couldn't convince Bill to try dialysis. He did accept hospice, and continued to tell me that he was feeling better each day until the day he died.

Living here enables me to take advantage of exercise sessions six days a week, and I do. The meals here are sometimes too good, but I've learned to stop eating when I feel filled, and to leave something on my plate is okay.

I have friends here around my age able to play with me the games I enjoy at least once a week, A bus is available here for professional appointments twice a week, and will take me shopping once a week.

Naomi's a Special Education teacher but still finds time to visit with me once a week. She told me she's proud that I still tutor reading students. I enjoy her company. We often go to the beauty shop, or for a massage, and sometimes we go to a play or a concert. She says she's glad I take good care of myself and hopes that I continue to do it for a long time because she's very busy and hasn't the time to learn how to handle my affairs. She's proud of me and says that I inspire her.

Ideally, it would be nice to have a healthy friend of the opposite sex to date occasionally, but I'm realistic and grateful to live one day at a time.

THE END

EPILOGUE

"Barschert" (Fate) is a word that more precisely describes the confluence of this event… It was meant to be!

That is the story of my life, both the bad and the good; the horrific memories of my early days and the joys of my later years. The accomplishments I've achieved as an adult were the result of the honing that occurred during my formative years.

The Cherokee Indians speak of two wolves within a child. One is angry and greedy. The other is peaceful and joyful.

Which one survives?

The one you feed.

BACK OF BOOK

One night, as Mama bathed me, I asked her why she didn't paint her nails?

"Who have you seen wearing nail polish?" she asked.

"The blonde lady Daddy takes me to see on Sunday."

After my parents' divorce, I overheard Grandma tell Mama, "Your baggage will hamper you finding a husband."

So, after Mama washed me that same night she said, "Don't call me Mama anymore."

Hearing this was very hurtful. My father hadn't taken me with him when he left. He went to live with his mother. Where could I go now? I felt Mama no longer wanted me either. I was four years old. Who would take care of me?

It was a desperate, sometime devastating journey through the depths of despair that I lived daily as a preschooler, and then a tumultuous adolescence with my malicious grandmother.

www.ingramcontent.com/pod-product-compliance
Lightning Source LLC
Chambersburg PA
CBHW060912120626
46553CB00001B/298